WISDOM IN THE STARS

WISDOM IN THE STARS

JOAN HODGSON

WHITE EAGLE PUBLISHING TRUST
NEW LANDS · LISS · HAMPSHIRE · ENGLAND

*First published by The White Eagle Lodge under
the name Joan Hodgson, July 1943
Second edition published by The White Eagle
Publishing Trust, September 1959
Third edition, June 1973
Fourth edition, February 2005*

*Cataloguing-in-Publication Data
A catalogue record for this publication is available
from the British Library*

ISBN 0-85487-159-4

Set in Baskerville and printed and bound by
Universal Packaging (Pvt) Ltd.
77, Nungamugoda Road,
Kelaniya, Sri Lanka

CONTENTS

FOREWORD

Joan Hodgson's book on the esoteric significance of the twelve signs of the zodiac has become a classic text in the sixty-odd years since it was first published. It was written, amazingly enough, in the middle of the Second World War, as a compilation of articles she had previously written for the White Eagle Lodge's magazine, then called ANGELUS. It remains as fundamentally important to the understanding of 'real' astrology today as it did then. Indeed, in all that time it has never been out of print.

The world has changed considerably since the mid-twentieth century. People live their lives at a much faster pace and the world has troubles of a different kind. Astrologers now do their calculations with computers. However, even the technologically-obsessed twenty-first-century world cannot alter the basic spiritual truths behind astrology which WISDOM IN THE STARS so clearly explains with such clarity.

For anyone willing to look beyond the superficial face of astrology, this is an ideal introduction to a subject that has occupied some of the greatest minds in the world for a very long time. It is no apology for its subject. On the contrary, it takes astrology's validity and truth for granted and sets out to explain to the reader what really lies behind those twelve great symbols known as the signs of the zodiac. At the same time, however, it is written in such an uncomplicated way that it can be understood by every interested reader. In fact, it might seem that the information in this book is especially aimed at those who have no prior knowledge of the subject. It takes the unnecessary mystery out of a discipline that has been surrounded with too much arcane information, presenting it as the logical, spiritual science that it truly is.

Simon Bentley, 2005

PUBLISHER'S PREFACE TO THE FOURTH EDITION

As the Foreword shows, this new edition can afford to celebrate a book which has been consistently in print for over sixty years. The number of revisions is larger than usual, removing a few archaisms and gender-specific pronouns. Simon Bentley, who has contributed the new Foreword, is the author's successor as Principal of the White Eagle School of Astrology. A short passage from White Eagle's teaching has been added at the end, and the reader of this book may well enjoy White Eagle's THE PATH OF THE SOUL after reading it.

INTRODUCTION

Our human lives are ordered by the stars and planets in their courses. Many people do not realize this fact, but there is an increasingly wide interest in astrology today. Some may regard astrology as superstitious nonsense, yet even as they argue, they demonstrate to the experienced astrologer by the very manner and substance of their speech, the planetary influences predominating in their birth charts.

Astrology falls into two categories. There is exoteric astrology, which can be seen at its most superficial level in the newspapers and magazines, and is chiefly concerned with light character analysis and the prediction of future trends in personal or national affairs. Predictions in the popular press are at a very lighthearted level and should not be taken seriously at all. It is impossible to make accurate general predictions based only on the Sun sign, and without any knowledge of the whole balance of the birth chart.

Esoteric astrology is quite a different matter. It is the study of the spiritual laws that guide the evolution of humanity, the spiritual principles which lie behind all material manifestation. Its basis is the universal law often mentioned in the Ancient Wisdom and known as the Law of Correspondences. It is simply expressed in the words, 'As above (in the heavens) so below (on earth); as below, so above.' To understand esoteric astrology, the student needs to understand and accept this spiritual law, together with the laws of reincarnation, karma (cause and effect), opportunity (that we are placed in the exact conditions which give the required opportunities for soul growth and development), and the law of balance or equilibrium, which causes the soul to pass through the opposing or balancing experiences of joy and sorrow, labour and rest, day and night—experiencing the constant ebb and flow of the tides of life.

Esoteric astrology is the study of the outworking of these great laws in human life in ways indicated by the planets and constellations. The gulf between this and exoteric astrology is as wide as the gulf that separates 'pop' music from a Beethoven symphony.

Fairytales, myths and legends the world over, as well as many of the familiar Bible stories, have their roots in astrology, which is in fact a science of religion: a spiritual science. Sincere students find it fascinating and absorbing, a constant source of inspiration and illumination, throwing light on all the deep human problems that confront human kind in their search for truth.

The human species is an intrinsic part of nature. The same life-processes that bring forth plant or animal also take place in each human being. Plant, bird, beast and human are alike dependent for existence upon the sun, the earth, the air, and the rain—as well as upon the interaction of the four elements, Fire, Earth, Air and Water. These elements provide food and nurture for our bodies and for those of all other created life—a fact that we accept as a matter of course because it is so obvious. However, it does not so readily occur to us that our souls may be likewise fed and nurtured by the spiritual counterpart of the four elements.

The laws which apply on earth also rule life in the heavens. Those laws which we term 'natural' can (with modifications) apply to both worlds. Astrology, or spiritual science, confirms this and teaches that the subtle fabric of our minds and souls is woven from finer spiritual elements, or ethers* which from the ancient days have been associated with the twelve signs of the zodiac. Each of these signs is said to 'belong' to a certain element; and as there are twelve signs equally distributed among the four elements, each element finds a threefold expression through the three signs allotted

*There is an interesting correlation here with the Hindu and yogic concept of 'sheaths' or kosas—Editor, 2005 edition

to it. That this threefold expression is analogous to the triune aspects of God, the Father–Mother–Son, or Wisdom–Love–Power aspects, is well known to students of astrology. This relationship will be further amplified in later chapters. The reader new to astrology should bear in mind that the signs of the zodiac fall into four groups of three, each group corresponding to one of the elements of Earth, Air, Fire or Water. The planets—by their known sympathy with certain signs—are also intimately connected with the elements.

During the Middle Ages, the idea of man or woman as a being composed of the four elements blended in varying proportions, and of his or her character and temperament being due to this blending, was universally held. In Shakespeare's *Julius Caesar* Mark Antony says of Brutus:

'His life was gentle, and the elements
So mixed in him that Nature might stand up
And say to all the world, 'This was a man!'

There are those that might scoff, but by studying a chart of the heavens as they appeared at the moment of a child's birth—the moment of the infant's first cry—a competent astrologer can obtain insight into a person's character and temperament, and go on to ascertain the physical make-up, the type of disease to which a person is likely to be subject, and to some degree, the nature of events that will influence a person's life. The skill and judgment that the astrologer shows in interpreting the blending of the elements shown by the signs of the zodiac and the planets are what make the delineation (the interpretation) of the chart more or less penetrating and accurate.

Although each of us receives influences from every sign or planet—or, in other words, although all the elements are combined in us, in most people one or another predominates and thus gives a temperament typical of that particular element. In medieval times these four temperaments, or 'humours' as they were called, formed the basis of medical treatment. Perhaps medical science will again realize one day the value of a knowledge of astrology in connection with healing.

In daily life, even without astrological knowledge, it is possible to gauge which of the elements predominates in our make-up or that of our friends. If the element Fire is predominant, they will be lovable, hasty, generous, somewhat hot-tempered, and enthusiastic about any person or project appealing to their imagination or their feelings. Often their hearts run away with their heads. In olden days, they would have been classed as having the 'choleric' (fiery) temperament. Being liable to feverish or inflammatory complaints, they would have been given soothing and cooling treatment.

On the other hand, we or some of our friends may possess what was known as the 'melancholic' (or earthy) temperament, and so will be placid, calm and collected, seldom moved to great excitement or enthusiasm; practical, capable, full of common sense, and excellently fitted to handle material problems, though seldom given to flights of fancy. Such people are most likely to suffer from complaints that arise from a clogging of the system, and need exercise and plenty of vital cleansing food and herbs.

People with an airy or 'sanguine' temperament, as the ancients called it, love refinement, beauty, and proportion and harmony of colour. Their homes will display their taste. They will be interested in reading and study, love to ponder over and discuss social, scientific or artistic problems, and often find theory more congenial than practice. Their health troubles generally come about through overstrained nerves or mental stress, and they need to learn mental control, thought-control.

Lastly, we come to the 'phlegmatic' temperament, in which the element Water plays the strongest part, this element being also connected with the body fluids. Its subjects are so sympathetic that they are inclined to bear the burdens of the world. They are also extremely psychic and receptive, and such sensitivity makes them difficult to understand, because they are apt to imagine slights where none are intended. When this happens, they become moody and sometimes sulky. They are timid and retiring, but when obliged to meet suffering, they display wonderful powers of endurance and tenacity. Their health troubles arise through exposure to chill and damp, and through impurities in diet or liquids, and they should exercise care in this respect.

As can be seen from these brief and very general descriptions, each element endows us with both virtues and failings. The purpose of our life here on earth is to learn so to understand and govern ourselves that we control the elements of our being, and can use them to the best advantage, instead of ourselves being used by them. Thus, we all need to learn to calm the waters of emotion and over-sensitivity, to control passion, irritability or excessive enthusiasm, and to curb destructive criticism resulting from ungoverned mental activity. When we do, we shall then learn that the outer elements of the physical world can obey our command as they did for the Master Jesus. We can look forward to being able to still our emotional tempest even as Jesus stilled the storm on the Sea of Galilee.

Self-control such as this, however, is not easy to acquire. It needs experience garnered in many incarnations before we learn to control even one of the elements. This is why we usually return to earth with the influence of one element predominating, so that during our lifetime we shall constantly absorb its lessons and undergo its tests. The majority of people meet this discipline unconsciously; more often than not they would deride the idea of being influenced and dominated in all their actions by unseen planetary vibrations in the ether; and yet the more materialistic and egoistic their outlook, the more completely do they respond to the pull of their stars. Any astrologer will confirm the fact that it is infinitely easier to predict events in the life of a spiritually-unawakened person than for one who understands spiritual values.

Socrates once said, 'Self-control is an exact science'. Any one who has studied astrology can recognize it as a science so closely linked to ourselves that by knowledge of the lore of the stars we can learn to know ourselves, and by gaining such knowledge in turn learn more of the greater mysteries of the universe.

Long, long ago, the mysteries of the lessons that needed to be learned by each human spirit were wrapped up in fairytales and fables. Even our Bible is full of similar allegories which, to those with eyes to see and ears to hear, unfold the heavenly secrets. These tests, which every soul undergoes before it attains mastery over the elements, are presented in fairytales as tasks, often seemingly impossible, which the hero or heroine must attempt. We have to realize that the dramatic quality of such tales is not confined to the imagination, but must work itself out wonderfully and surely in every human life. In very truth, every soul is a hero embarked upon an arduous quest, as glorious and as exacting as that undertaken for the Holy Grail.

Having considered astrology in a general sense, we are now ready to study the influence of the signs of the zodiac, the constellations and the planets in greater detail. It would perhaps be helpful if we first outline the basic principles upon which all astrological teachings are founded.

Physical science teaches us that in our universe the sun, a fixed star, threw off in turn the planets that form the solar system. It remains the source of all life on earth. Spiritual science amplifies this statement, by saying that the physical sun is sign and symbol of a greater spiritual sun, symbolic of God the Father—who is also both Mother and Creator—and that within each human being there dwells a living spark of God, like a tiny sun or fixed star. In the course of development this also throws off or builds for itself different vehicles or higher bodies, each bearing intimate relationship with one of the solar planets; and each higher body is more or less contained in or interpenetrates the physical body.

17

This teaching helps us to understand the biblical statement that God created men and women in His–Her own image and likeness. If God is like the sun, with the solar universe as one of His–Her vehicles of manifestation, then man–woman (God's temple) is also like a sun (although a dim and minute one); one who must also learn to create, control, and perfect his–her own universe. Thus, we may see the microcosm evolving and developing within the macrocosm, subject to the same laws and endowed with the same glorious possibilities. For all we know, our physical universe—to us so vast—may yet be but an infinitesimal part of some vaster, grander cosmos beyond the comprehension of our frail human minds. Even so, its mystery can be no greater than the mystery of our own being, for

'The without is like the within of things; the small is like the large; there is only one Law, and He who works is One. In the divine economy there is neither great nor small. Men are mortal gods, and gods are immortal men.' (Fragment of Hermes.)

The light of love, which shines as a sun within the heart of every human being, is one with the Great Architect of the Universe, and possesses power to order human life with the same harmony and perfection as is manifested by the stars in their courses. Did not Jesus exhort his disciples, *Be ye therefore perfect, even as your Father which is in heaven is perfect?*

The majority of us, however, are very far from even glimpsing this perfection within ourselves; and although we wistfully contemplate the grandeur of the heavens, we find it difficult to identify ourselves with the God power, the Architect within, which will enable us to fashion order out of chaos.

To help the Sun, the Christ within us, to develop full self-consciousness, we descend to the earth plane along with millions of other 'infant suns', to learn through that experience which we gain chiefly through our national, social and family relationships with these other suns. Thus do we grow in wisdom, love and power.

It seems a far cry from our puny human relationships to those of the Sun and the other fixed stars in the heavens—and yet is the idea too fantastic? 'As above, so below'—and if we who are suns in the making can be moulded and modified by our environment and especially by our close associates, may it not also be that a matching mutual relationship exists between the stars?

As we know, the Sun is not the only fixed star, and is by no means the largest. Around and about it are myriads of other fixed stars, constellations and nebulae (stars in the making,) some of which we can observe on a clear night. Most of these stars are probably suns, ruling universes of which we with our limited consciousness can have no conception. Astrology teaches, however, that between our Sun and these other stars exists a relationship which manifests to us on earth through the twelve signs of the zodiac.

As the earth travels in her yearly orbit round the Sun, the latter appears to us to be shining against the ever-changing background of constellations. We know, of course, that it is the earth that moves, and not the Sun. But to an observer on earth, it appears that our earth is the stationary body, while the Sun apparently circles round us. We can mark and measure its progress by means of the constellations and fixed stars forming its background. We also see the planets moving against this background, and the pathway which they appear to follow round the earth is known as the 'circle of the zodiac'. This circle is divided into twelve sections called 'signs of the zodiac', which are named after the constellations most closely associated with them. The following old rhyme shows the signs in order, beginning with Aries (the Ram), which the Sun enters on the first day of spring.

The Ram, the Bull, the Heavenly Twins,
And next the Crab, the Lion shines,
    The Virgin and the Scales,
The Scorpion, Archer and the Goat,

The Man who bears the Watering Pot,
    And the Fish with glittering tails.

These signs, named after constellations, can be likened to our environmental circle—the circle of friends, relatives and associates who modify and influence our own lives. Each month, the Sun enters a different sign of the zodiac. As it does so, the quality of the spiritual power and light that it pours forth onto the earth becomes modified and changed because of its magnetic or spiritual contact with other stars in its environmental circle. It is similar to the way in which we show forth a different aspect of our being according to whether we contact a distant acquaintance, a teacher or a pupil, a member of our family or a dear friend. The same principle applies to the solar planets, whose influences are modified by the sign of the zodiac in which they are placed.

As has been stated, each sign is related to one of the four elements; and the angels of these elements play an important part in the education of every individual, from the moment when each being is breathed forth, a minute spark of God-life. The newborn spirit remains for a time in the Garden of Eden (or of innocence), and while in this state is conscious only of security and bliss within the care of the Father–Mother God. It has no sense of separateness, or of individuality.

When the period of infancy is past, however, having 'eaten of the tree of the knowledge of good and evil' (or, in other words, having become conscious of itself as a separate entity), it must of necessity explore the possibilities of its own powers. It has to grapple with the shadow-substances of matter, and to do that it has to descend completely into the darkness of earth.

The pure, bright flame of God, which forms the human spirit, cannot immediately become clothed in that matter which forms the normal physical body. As it descends through the spheres it must build for itself vehicles of subtler matter, each vehicle or body in turn vibrating more slowly until the dense physical body is reached. Thus, the pure spirit is well-protected by many coverings.

The time of incarnation is chosen by each human spirit so that the planetary and zodiacal conditions are such as to ensure that the 'raw materials' for building the various vehicles are supplied by the devas (or angels) of the four elements in the exact proportions required for learning certain lessons. Those who find it difficult to reconcile this conception of human freewill with astrological predestination should remember that while the devas (working through the signs of the zodiac) supply the raw materials, the spirit must be its own architect. At first it finds great difficulty in handling the materials.

Many experiments must be made, and periods of trial and error passed through, before mastery is gained. Consequently, in young and inexperienced souls the higher vehicles have hardly any shape or form, and to the eye of the trained seer appear nebulous and cloud-like, since the spirit has yet to mould and refine the 'raw materials' into instruments which perfectly express its Godlike powers.

The mastery of each element presents a different problem to the human spirit, a problem which with its three phases is designed eventually to call forth the divine attributes of Wisdom, Love and Power, and to enable these to manifest through every aspect of being. The following paragraphs may help us to understand this.

The element Fire teaches the lesson of love, its power, mystery, and magic. Souls learning to master this element will encounter many experiences designed to show them the true meaning of love. When they discover its secret power, they must also learn wisdom. Love is the magic fire, the flame on the altars of the gods, which cleanses, purifies, heals and inspires, but when used without wisdom can be an instrument of destruction.

The element Earth is concerned with helping the human spirit to gain mastery over physical matter, and teaches the practical lesson of service. Those who return to earth to learn this lesson may often appear absorbed in material life and to have no time for spiritual aspiration—a natural phase through which all souls pass at some period in their development. Not until this spiritual darkness of absorption in matter has been experienced does aspiration towards the Light awaken. The soul learning the lessons of Earth will begin to study the spiritual laws of the cosmos as the means of expressing its desire to be more efficient in practical service. In striving after spiritual truth, we sometimes ignore the practical aspects of life. The element Earth teaches us that true spiritual development must also bring increased practical efficiency, or *mastery over physical matter.* The universe would be in a sad state were not the laws of God precise and perfect in every material detail.

Air, the element through which the quickening sunlight and the refreshing rain succour the earth, teaches the lesson of brotherhood. Of all the four, Air is the most subtle element and best blends and harmonizes with the others. The great quality which the Air devas pass on to those studying the lessons of this element, is dispassion: the ability to stand aside, to observe and to learn from the interplay of human lives and personalities. When this quality manifests in an inexperienced soul, it often causes superiority and mental arrogance.

This is because, living in the world of his or her own mind, and governed largely by reason, the person is rarely if ever moved to ill-considered action, and has little sympathy or respect for those who are. All who are learning the lesson of the element Air must overcome the tendency to allow their gift of dispassion to manifest as 'splendid isolation,' but should cultivate true brotherhood with others, recognizing both their weaknesses and strength, while remaining unmoved by petty slights, hurts and jealousies.

The lesson which the element Water teaches the human spirit is control of the emotions, so that peace can be found. Since the astral and emotional vehicles are largely built of this element, those who return to earth to learn this lesson are much swayed by feeling and emotion. Their sympathies will flow out to all, while they themselves are most sensitive and easily hurt. Their problem is how to control these tempestuous passions and emotions so that they can hold themselves in such a state of equilibrium that 'the Spirit of God' can 'move on the face of the waters,' and call the true life of the spirit into being.

We can discover which of these four lessons we have to learn in our present incarnation by studying the sign of the zodiac in which the Sun was placed at the time of our birth. We can tell this from the date of the birthday.

A list of the dates at which the Sun is passing through each sign, showing the element and lesson associated with its position, is given below:

Typical date	Sun Sign	Element	Lesson
March 21 to April 20	Aries	Fire	Love
April 20 to May 2 1	Taurus	Earth	Service
May 2 1 to June 22	Gemini	Air	Brotherhood
June 22 to July 23	Cancer	Water	Peace
July 23 to August 23	Leo	Fire	Love
August 23 to Sept 23	Virgo	Earth	Service
Sept 23 to Oct 24	Libra	Air	Brotherhood
Oct 24 to Nov 22	Scorpio	Water	Peace
Nov 22 to Dec 22	Sagittarius	Fire	Love
Dec 22 to Jan 21	Capricorn	Earth	Service
Jan 21 to Feb 20	Aquarius	Air	Brotherhood
Feb 20 to March 21	Pisces	Water	Peace

People born between the 20th and the 24th of any month are in a transition stage. Their period of apprenticeship under the previous sign is almost over for the time being, and they are approaching the following sign, so that the experiences of life will be to some extent a blending of the lessons of two elements.

In the chapters that follow, we shall deal with the lessons of each sign in detail, showing how the ancient myths and fairytales were in many cases designed as parables to help the evolving human soul to understand the inner truths of his or her own being.

ARIES

The Sun enters the sign of Aries every year on the first day of spring, which can be regarded from an astrological viewpoint as a New Year's Day, since this sign is usually considered to be the first in the circle of the zodiac. During the month that follows the first day of spring, new life surges into being. Grass, flower and tree awaken to the spring sunshine, birds and animals bring forth their young, and the whole period is rich and vibrant with new young life.

Such activity is typical of the sign of Aries, in which the element Fire manifests in what is known as its cardinal phase. As has been mentioned, each element possesses three distinct modes, or phases of activity. We might compare these phases, first, to an outpouring of energy from some primary, eternal source; secondly, to a stabilization or organization of that energy; and, finally, when the purpose of the initial outpouring is served, a returning to the source from which it came. These three aspects form an essential rhythm of life such as occurs in all natural processes: in the growth and decay of plants, the ebb and flow of the tides, and even in the blood-circulation of the human body.

It is interesting to note that the Sun enters the sign associated with the cardinal, outpouring, or most active phase of each element, at the turn of a season. Thus, at the beginning of spring it enters the cardinal Fire sign of Aries; at the beginning of summer, the cardinal Water sign of Cancer; at the beginning of autumn, the cardinal Air sign of Libra; and at the beginning of winter, the cardinal Earth sign of Capricorn. The stabilizing and organizing aspect is associated with the fixed signs, Taurus, Leo, Scorpio and Aquarius, which the Sun enters as a season reaches its height. The returning aspect, that of wisdom and adaptation, is shown by the mutable signs, Gemini, Virgo, Sagittarius and Pisces, occupied by the Sun at the period of each season's change and decline.

The sign of Aries, then, shows the element Fire in its fiercest or most energetic phase. For a symbolic picture of the qualities of the sign, we cannot do better than to visualize the flames of a newly-lit fire, leaping from coal to coal or from log to log in a grate; or, uncontrolled, a prairie fire roaring onwards, relentless, purposeful and indiscriminate. Fire can be a warm, friendly, satisfying blaze, a beacon light to lonely travellers, a protection against wild, unfriendly things; but also a fury of destruction if uncontrolled.

The lesson which the element Fire teaches is love; and as Aries manifests the power, or action-phase of this element, the particular lesson which souls must learn who were born between March 21st and April 20th, when the Sun is in this sign, is the wise use of love. Many incarnations must pass before a soul learns the full meaning of love, and few at present understand its magical power, referred to in fairytale and legend as the magic sword which can vanquish the fiercest enemies. In actual life, however, each individual becomes the hero of his or her own fairytale: a tale which symbolizes the unfoldment of his or her spirit, not merely during one incarnation, but throughout the whole cycle of individual evolution. Everyone must eventually earn this magic sword of perfect love which can slay the enemy, fear; and vanquish not only all external foes, but those of the inmost self: depression, jealousy and unkindness.

Two famous legends in which the magic sword figures prominently are the English Arthurian saga and that of the German Siegfried, which Wagner has immortalized. Although these stories naturally show many differences, there is one striking similarity. In each case, the hero's own sword is shattered, and he is provided with a new one. (In the case of Siegfried, the broken sword is mended by magical power.) This broken sword, and the provision of a new, invincible sword has a special significance for those born with the Sun in Aries. That is because in this incarnation the fire and enthusiasm within their spirit rush them headlong into physical, mental, or emotional expression, causing them to try to storm their objective—whether it be a person, an idea or an ideal. Sometimes this enthusiasm carries all before it; and the object once achieved, happiness or misery is reaped, according to the wisdom and discrimination behind the desire. Often, however, the energy, boldness and determination of the spirit come up against an even stronger power, the Law of God; and then this mortal sword of desire breaks into fragments and the soul is left disconsolate. Thus, children of Aries find that again and again they work with all the enthusiasm, courage and ardour of their being, only to find the object of their endeavours worthless, or to be denied it by an apparently malevolent stroke of destiny.

Whenever the sword forged from the iron of selfish desire (on any plane of being) is shattered, the soul is forced to pause and to reflect. After painful experience, realization gradually dawns that whenever the outrush of love and enthusiasm is tinged with self, all the heroism and energy expended is wasted … the sword made by human hands must always break. Thus, the soul is brought face to face with the truth that of itself and for itself alone it can do nothing.

When this awareness dawns, the soul ceases to follow every ardent impulse, but quietly ascertains if its selfwill is in harmony with the divine Will. With newborn humility and resignation there comes a change. The fire which before flashed fitfully, or with wild impetuosity, now becomes governed and restrained and manifests as love, pure and ardent. Thus, being freed from taint of self, it can no longer experience hurt or disillusionment; it becomes as love burning with a bright, steady flame, a sword of light, an Excalibur ready for the soul to reach out to and grasp. The magic of this sword of love cannot be withstood; it opens barred doors, heals wounds, and scatters shadow and illusion. In other words, selfless love welling up within the heart becomes as a flaming sword that strengthens and protects the mind against every onslaught of evil: *Perfect love casteth out fear.*

The symbolism of the story of Siegfried differs from that of King Arthur, for here the sword is broken when Siegmund, the hero's father, infringes the Law in pursuit of his own desires. The latter dies, but his son welds the shattered fragments into a weapon more potent than ever. This is another illustration of the age-old truths of which Jesus spoke: *Except ye be born again of water and the spirit ye shall in no wise enter the kingdom of heaven.* In

33

Siegfried, Siegmund was reborn, and with the former selfish attitude to life buried , he was at last able to wield the magic sword.

Aries, the Ram, is also the symbol of sacrifice. Old Testament stories many times refer to the sacrifice of the ram on the altar. In the New Testament, however, especially in the Book of Revelation, Christ is symbolized as the Lamb of God who takes away the sins of the world. Though a different symbol, this demonstrates the same truth as the magic sword. The old ram represents the 'old Adam'—that selfish, arrogant and worldly self which has to be sacrificed on the altar of divine love. In its place arises the pure white Lamb of God, the gentle but all powerful Christ-consciousness which is the saviour of human kind.

In the northern hemisphere, the Sun enters this sign when all nature rejoices in a new birth, when the power of the arisen life-force has triumphed over the darkness and icy grip of winter. The lesson, then, which all children of Aries must learn is that of putting aside the old self, which wields in vain the sword of desire; and of putting on the new self which understands and uses the true magic of selfless love. Thus shall they show forth in their lives the real meaning of the sign of Aries, which is the power of the arisen Christ.

TAURUS

The Sun enters the sign of Taurus each year around April 20th. During its passage through this sign, the northern world becomes clothed with the beauty of the early flowers and fresh spring leaves. We have only to stand silently in a wood with senses alert to become aware of the life-force, the new spirit pulsating within mother nature, quickening and moulding all things into grace and beauty. When the Sun is in Aries, this fresh outpouring of life-force becomes evident, but when it passes through the sign of Taurus, the manifestation of the newly-arisen life in matter is complete. Perhaps this is why in ancient days this sign was considered to represent in a general sense the physical body, which the enshrined spirit should govern and illumine.

Taurus belongs to the element Earth, which here manifests in its fixed mode, and forms perhaps the most stable, practical sign of the zodiac. All the Earth signs are concerned with matter, through which the spirit must learn to work, and Earth in its fixed phase

shows matter at its densest. Therefore we are not sur-
prised to discover that Taurus largely rules money and
possessions, two factors which can hold both rich and
poor firmly down to earth. Unless we have had long
training in spiritual discipline, it is not easy to aspire to
spiritual heights if we are hungry and our creditors are
dogging us. Neither can we serve others if our bodies
are clogged and diseased through over-indulgence or
if we live in constant worry lest anything should hap-
pen to our possessions. Both extremes chain us down
irretrievably, and give us little time for or interest in the
reality of spirit. Even if we do not indulge in extremes,
the so-called practical aspect of life undoubtedly forces
us to remember that while we are 'of the earth, earthy'
we need material sustenance.

As previously stated, the lesson which the Earth devas
would teach human kind is that of service, on all planes,
in all its aspects. Because of our physical dependencies,
we soon realize that if we serve others faithfully according to our gifts and capacity, they in turn will help us.
Nature herself demonstrates that if we exert ourselves
to plough, sow and cultivate, she will in turn bring forth
abundantly. Thus if we want food, clothing, home and
possessions we must earn them by effort, by service
in some form or another, either to mother earth or to
other human beings.

The fixed Earth sign of Taurus teaches us this lesson very practically, first on the physical plane. This is why we often find souls under its influence immersed and absorbed in business and finance, or in pleasure and luxury, toiling unremittingly to acquire the wealth and possessions which they think ensure them physical comfort and security; and neglecting anything that does not lead to this practical end. On the other hand, if they are in a position where they can enjoy comfort and ease without struggle and toil, they happily settle down into a routine existence, and nothing short of an earthquake, or stark physical necessity, will move them to effort.

Venus, the planet of beauty, harmony and pleasure, is the ruler of the sign of Taurus We can easily realize, therefore, how an inherent love of beauty and harmony, which Venus brings, can manifest in inexperienced souls coming under this sign as desire for bodily comfort and luxury. A baby first learns to realize its separateness from its mother by discovery of and delight in its own physical faculties. Similarly, the young soul must first learn of itself by becoming absorbed in interests immediately surrounding and associated with its material body and environment. All souls traverse this necessary stage of evolution—when they labour or give service—only because the needs of the body and lower self are thereby supplied.

The bull or ox is the symbol of the sign, and the golden calf worshipped by the Israelites in the wilderness is still idolized by the inexperienced children of Taurus. Mammon dazzles them; they are like the mythical King Midas, who wished that everything he touched should turn into gold. Often the Taurean possesses so good a business instinct that he or she wins such success with ease. Then he or she also must learn the lesson of Midas: that gold, while valuable and right in its proper place, forms but a poor substitute for the food of the spirit, and for the love and companionship of others.

In this way the Earth devas, especially of this fixed Earth sign, chain the spirit to matter. It is indeed a blessing that as we descend into physical bodies in order to learn our lessons we receive the gift of forgetfulness of the Garden of Eden. We only vaguely yearn for some ideal existence of which our innermost heart informs us, a vision which the mind stifles and calls imagination. Once the young soul has revelled to the full in physical sensation, has experienced both poverty and wealth (or the denial and fulfilment of material ambition), it begins to wonder about the purpose of its existence. At first, a child given wax or potter's clay to model with enjoys the physical sensation of pushing, punching and squeezing its material into fantastic shapes. After a while, when the little fingers have become more accustomed, the creative urge begins to manifest. The child now wants to mould and form the clay into recognizable form. In the same way, the human 'baby-spirit' first plays with and experiments with the physical life and its natural resources. Then the will and the creative power of the higher mind begin to create order out of chaos, and to mould the temple of the body and the soul into form and beauty.

In ancient days, the element Earth was always represented as a perfect cube, a form ready for building into a temple. Souls learning the lesson of Taurus are endeavouring to attain to precision and perfection, not only on the physical plane (where they are usually most painstaking and steady) but also in their soul-life. Carefully and steadily every soul must work to gain control over the physical and lower self, so that instead of imprisoning the spirit, the body glorifies and serves it. Taurus is the sign of the builder, and while this is true on the material plane, it is even more so on the inner planes. In giving service to others on the outer plane of life, the soul is unconsciously building and perfecting the temple of its own being. Furthermore, it is clearing away unwanted corners and excrescences, moulding and shaping itself until, like the perfect cube, it fits into its appointed place in the great temple of the universe.

In myths and fairytales, we often read of houses, palaces, cities, built by magical power. Rome and Troy were supposed to have been created by the power of music so rhythmic and so harmonious that the stones moved of their own accord into position. The story of Aladdin, who discovered, deep down in a cavern, a wonderful lamp with powers to build him fairy palaces, typifies longings which might be brought into being by some such magical power. These fairy stories embody not idle fancies, but symbolic and even scientific reality. There does exist a magical power: one which, when discovered and utilized, will build not only body and soul, but will shape the actual stones of the material world into beauty.

This power, like Aladdin's lamp, is buried deep within the heart of nature, and also deep within the heart of all people. It can heal us when we are wounded or sick; it is the power behind all life and growth: the power of Christ, the Sun. We are slothful, and as in Aladdin's case a long time passes for us before we begin to discover the magical properties of this God-given power. As soon as we trust it and follow its guidance, our vision opens. Simple and unselfish love can work miracles, but how often we forget to rub the little lamp and liberate the genie! If the immediate results should appear ordinary and commonplace we do not persist. We expect the fairy palaces to appear instantly, even before we have rubbed the lamp clean and bright.

Yet surely, as we persist, as we endeavour to let love colour our whole attitude not only towards other people, but towards life and all its circumstances, we shall find the power at work, first manifesting as increasing health in our physical body. Then, almost simultaneously, we shall develop the ability to give healing to others. Love implies harmony and understanding; and if we love all life, we shall endeavour to understand and bring ourselves and others into harmony. The more we bring ourselves into harmony with natural law, into attunement with the harmony of the universe, the nearer we come to the magic secret of Aladdin's lamp—or of Apollo's lyre, the music of which raised the walls of Troy.

This secret is one all children of Taurus are working to discover. The fair palaces, so often hidden and forgotten, must be brought forth. To do this a soul calls to its aid the 'genies', the hidden powers of nature, the angels of form and beauty. Every endeavour on the material plane adds symmetry and beauty to the temple some day to be inhabited by the soul in the life beyond, for there is no separation between the here and the 'over there'. The two are interlinked.

Venus, the planet of harmony, of love, of beauty and music, is the ruler of Taurus, the sign of the builder;

for in creating a temple for the soul surely only perfection is good enough? Children of Taurus should strive continually against the spiritual indolence that beset Aladdin, and mould the clay of earthliness into beauty, so that every detail of home, business, or workshop is conducted with precision, justice and perfection. *Be ye therefore perfect, even as your Father which is in heaven is perfect.*

GEMINI

About May 21st each year, the Sun enters the sign of
Gemini, the Heavenly Twins. At this time, the fresh
radiance of springtime is imperceptibly giving place
to the maturity of summer; spring blossoms are nearly
over, while the summer flowers have yet to reach their
prime. Nature is passing through a transition period that
corresponds to the sign of the zodiac from which the
Sun's rays will fall on the earth for the next month. The
mutable phase of an element is always one of change,
adaptation and transmutation, and Gemini manifests
this phase of the element Air.

While Taurus and the Earth signs promote development of the spirit through its control over matter,
Gemini and the Air signs call forth the faculty of
thought and the unfoldment of the mental vehicles.
Without this power, experience in matter would be of
little value, for we should lack memory and the ability
to reason and experiment in order to discover the most
harmonious way of life through knowledge of good and

evil. Through the development of its mental vehicles, a soul learns to co-operate consciously with natural forces which will bring mastery over matter. Such conscious cooperation, or brotherhood, is the lesson which all children of the Air signs, Gemini, Libra and Aquarius, are endeavouring to learn. It is interesting to notice that each of these signs in some way influences our co-operation with others, for Gemini has general rulership over brothers, sisters and cousins; Libra over the marriage or business partner (also enemies and rivals); and Aquarius over friends and associates.

Gemini, the first of the Air signs, rules the equipment whereby a man or woman is enabled to become aware of his or her environment, to reason about his or her experiences, and to communicate a conscious reactions to others. This equipment comprises the brain and nervous system, which sensitize and direct the whole body. It controls the power of speech, whereby ideas and thoughts can be communicated to others through discussion, lectures, education, and so forth. It also directs the hands, which are among the chief agents of the brain, permitting communication through writing and gesture. All these are associated with Gemini. It may be observed that the mutable signs have the quality of extreme flexibility, which, in the case of the Air element, falls under the rulership of the planet Mercury, whose metal is quicksilver. The brain and nerves, especially those of the fingers, need the volatile response of quicksilver if they are to penetrate successfully the denseness of physical life and convey impressions to and directions from the spirit.

In Greek mythology, Mercury is the inventor of the lyre, the stringed instrument from which Apollo, the Sun god, drew indescribably beautiful music. In human kind, the mercurial influence is gradually refining and perfecting the subtler mental bodies, together with the nervous system, until they become like a perfect instrument through which true communication between earth and heaven may be established. Mercury was the winged messenger of the gods, and every man and woman will eventually, through Mercury's power, develop such a fine, sensitive coordination of the higher vehicles with the physical brain, that every individual's thoughts will be winged and their lives will manifest the music of the spheres.

When the inexperienced soul descends into incarnation, the range of its consciousness (particularly while in the physical body) is very limited, and its reasoning powers underdeveloped. Its actions are largely motivated by instincts and impulses welling up from subconscious mental levels. The moral sense, or knowledge of good and evil, in this area of the mind is very slight.

In the average person, the field of daily consciousness is extremely limited, compared with the unexplored realms of the subconscious and the superconscious mind, which regulate much of his or her life. As we grow in spiritual age and experience, however, our mercurial flexibility of mind and nerves increases, also our sensitivity to impression and expression. The field of our consciousness expands until we learn to understand not only the outer world but the secrets of our own being. When the realms of the subconscious and the superconscious mind are fully explored, and their hidden powers brought into conscious use, the spirit can manifest in full power on all planes of being.

As its name indicates, Gemini, or the Heavenly Twins, is a dual sign. It symbolizes the dual cosmic forces, positive and negative, good and evil, light and darkness, which the soul must learn to understand and master before it can reach its goal, divine wisdom. The human mind is similar to quicksilver, which responds to every change in atmospheric pressure. How quickly our mercury sinks when we read, see or hear anything depressing; how quickly it rises when some incident elates us. Souls strongly influenced by Gemini are very responsive to mental impression. They are passing through a phase during which the mental vehicles are being quickened and sensitized, and would do well to meditate on the inner meaning of the myth of Castor and Pollux, the Heavenly Twins. Castor, who was mortal, was killed in battle; but Pollux, being immortal, was allowed to restore his brother to life—provided that he agreed to descend from heaven to spend half his time in the underworld.

Our minds, like Castor and Pollux, are dual. One half, being mortal, is receptive to negative impressions such as depression, fear, unkindness and worry. The other, immortal half, is responsive to the positive vibrations of love, light, joy and peace. Almost daily, Castor, the negative or lower mind, is overcome, or 'slain', by fears, worries and problems. Yet in every one of us waits the other twin, Pollux, ready to save Castor. However, for most of us, our willpower is so undeveloped that we allow the negative aspect of life to hold full sway, instead of resolutely turning towards that good and positive thought which will lift poor, much-scarred Castor into the Light. When we allow Pollux, or our superconscious mind, to operate in daily life, then during our sleep the lower, conscious mind, Castor, will learn gradually to migrate to the heaven world for recreation, and we shall remember on waking the beautiful experiences which have been ours.

Souls learning the lesson of Gemini will find the duality of the sign manifesting in many ways. The mind

47

develops and learns to reason by comparing and clas-
sifying different types of experience, discovering their
differences and their similarities, and through these
observations deciding on the wisest course of future
action. Where lies the consciousness of good or evil
but in our minds? Our bodies, unless firmly controlled and guided by the wisdom we have acquired, obey
the dictates of instinct and habit. Our emotions, often
far more unmanageable, make almost an automatic
response to stimulus from without; but our minds remember, observe and compare. They gradually store up
experience, which enables us to decide upon our course
of action. That which brings lasting joy and peace we
learn to regard as right and good, while that which
brings pain we regard as wrong. As soon as this wisdom
of experience becomes ingrained within us, no doubt
remains as to which path we should choose. Advice and
warning from others often prove of little value, for until
we ourselves have experienced the sensations of being
burnt or frozen, how can we realize the value of fire
when wisely used and controlled?

Inexperienced souls incarnating under Gemini often
appear fickle, changeable, unreliable, and sometimes
amoral. When a soul is young, its first lessons need to
be simple and clear. If it returns to earth with the object
of quickening its mental faculties, it can concentrate on

one aspect of life alone, and cannot at this stage deal with emotional or other complexities. It therefore seeks many and varied experiences, which will sharpen the mind, make it flexible, and give it material for observation, comparison and the exercise of its reasoning powers. Young Geminian souls often show surprising lack of feeling and emotional depth, with little or no concentration and staying power; but they develop much intellectual dexterity, cunning and sleight of hand, and are past masters at wriggling out of a difficult situation. Mercury was known to the ancients as the 'god of thieves.'

Each time the cycle of development brings the soul again to the lesson of Gemini, the background of knowledge and experience grows wider, the emotions richer and more mature. Gradually the quickening mental powers turn towards the deeper problems of humanity and the universe. Souls are drawn to the study of the arts and sciences, and to a deeper understanding of the eternal pair of opposites which manifests through all life. They will learn the secret of co-operation with these forces, so that each serves its proper purpose, in the same way as the electrician makes use of the positive and negative electrical currents. This co-operation will extend not only to the material and natural forces, but to principles active within themselves and all human beings.

For in every soul the twin brothers of mind, Castor and Pollux, are at work, rendering the soul responsive to negative, evil and unkindly, or to positive, good and kindly thought. As we become more sensitive, alert and responsive, we shall notice how by our thought, speech and actions we can easily call forth either one of the twin brethren in others, and we shall learn to strengthen Pollux, the immortal, so that the mortal or lower mind will be irradiated and redeemed.

This is the art of brotherhood, which all children of Gemini are learning. It is their duty, whether their gifts find expression through speech, writing, or the work of their hands, so to live that they constantly call forth the divine brother–sister in others.

The Romans believed that whenever the twin brethren were seen at the helm of a ship at sea, it was a sure sign of a safe and successful voyage. This symbol is as true for the soul today as in days of old; as soon as our minds are truly poised and polarized, as soon as Pollux has raised Castor to immortality, the twin brethren, divine Wisdom and Intelligence are at the helm, and our true course is set; or, to change our metaphor, we enter through the twin pillars into the temple of the universe and are led to the garden where grows the tree of life.

CANCER

The Sun usually enters the Water sign of Cancer on June 22nd. This date also marks an important event in the seasonal phenomena—the summer solstice, the day on which the Sun reaches the most northerly point of its journey, and which in the northern hemisphere we know as the longest day. A few days later, on June 24th, occurs a festival day almost as important as Christmas: Midsummer Day. Indeed, Midsummer Day holds the same significance for the southern hemisphere as does Christmas for the northern; because long before the birth of Jesus the ancient peoples welcomed the return of the 'newborn' Sun, which brought the promise of spring and summer, of life renewed. When the southern hemisphere welcomes 'the newborn King,' the northern hemisphere at midsummer bids him farewell. Most of the ancient races, including those in Britain, led by their priests, held sacred festivals on both occasions, the Christmas festival being the welcome and the midsummer the farewell to the Sun. At the latter, praise and thanksgiving were offered for blessings received, and the help of the devas of the four elements and the spirits of the nature kingdom were invoked to ensure a good harvest. This is probably why stories and legends about the power of the fairies on midsummer eve abound in British folklore.

The element Water, to which the sign of Cancer belongs, when woven into the fabric of human life and consciousness, gives rise to that most delicate, receptive and vulnerable aspect of our being, the feelings and emotions. Of all the elements, water is the most absorbent and receptive. Not only does it absorb, purify and dissolve all manner of substances, but it reflects every mood, every colour and movement in the world about it. The devas of this element are particularly concerned with the human response to feeling and sensation, and with the development of psychic and emotional vehicles. We find, therefore, that children of the Water signs, no matter what their evolutionary stage, are extremely sensitive, receptive and impressionable; so much so, that they are apt to feel too keenly the harshness of material life, and have to adopt some method of self-protection.

As has been previously mentioned, the ultimate aim of the spirit when incarnating under the influence of the element Water, is to learn the lesson of peace: not a sluggish, apathetic condition, the result of retreat from the fray and concealment, but poise of mind, soul and spirit which, while giving relaxation and inward stillness, is dynamic in its recuperative and energizing power. This lesson is only learnt after the soul has touched the heights and depths of emotional and sensational experience. Until the secret of this inward serenity is discovered, various methods of self-protection are tried, according to which of the three signs exerts most influence during the particular incarnation. Natives of the sign of Scorpio feel that attack is the best form of defence, and so they develop the sting of the scorpion in speech, manner or action at the first sign of any real or imagined unfriendliness. On the other hand, the children of Pisces more often seek an escape, and either live in an imaginary world of their own creation, or dull their senses with drugs or alcohol. The influence of Cancer, the Crab, causes its children to seek the protection of their own environment and to build around themselves a shell of reserve guarding them from strangers or enemies. Souls born with this sign emphasized in their horoscopes are natural home-lovers. They have a special need for the security and protection of a harmonious home environment.

In Cancer, the element Water manifests in its cardinal, or active, energetic phase. Natives of the sign show attributes of the element that are vigorous and progressive. For instance, the absorbent quality of water reveals itself in an inherent love of collecting and storing up against future need, so that the 'shell' contains sufficient sustenance to outlast many a rainy day. In unevolved souls this tendency often leads to miserliness or extreme meanness; in most people it manifests as caution, prudence and a careful husbanding of resources. On the other hand, the advanced soul develops the ability to draw upon the cosmos for spiritual food and sustenance, which in turn is distributed, not only to intimates, but to a much wider circle. In a more general sense, the sign of Cancer represents that aspect of the spirit which collects and absorbs the experiences, the feelings and sensations of many lives. These experiences gradually build the individuality, which we may here define as the permanent temple of the spirit. It is the composite soul body, the wedding garment of the spirit. Because it is built up through so many life-experiences, it can be compared to Joseph's coat of many colours.

In ancient Egypt the symbol of the sign was a little hard-shelled beetle known as a scarab, and this was also regarded as representing the psyche, or soul. The conception of the shell of protection to cover the tender, vulnerable receptive feelings is significant. No soul is perfected, no spirit reaches the state of mastership until, built into the aura through the wisdom, love and power gained by much experience, is a complete circle of Light, a silver shield which surrounds and protects the soul from all ill. Within this circle or 'egg' of Light the soul remains poised and radiant, able to send forth spiritual power and succour those in need, and yet allowing no darkness or disturbing influence to enter his or her sanctuary. The unevolved soul instinctively endeavours to form this protective shield, but limited by youth and inexperience, its efforts result in self-centredness, narrowness of outlook, clannishness, and lack of interest in anything that does not concern its immediate environment.

It must be remembered, however, that the sign of Cancer manifests the cardinal, or energetic, active phase of the element Water, and that its planetary ruler is the Moon, the great Mother. In children of this sign, therefore, the feelings and emotions must find active expression in spite of the innate timidity and sensitivity characteristic of the Water element. Out of this rises a strong maternal instinct, which desires to protect, to shield, and to store up sustenance not only for the self but for anything which is loved and helpless. When the soul is young, this protective maternal love can only enfold a small circle. Sometimes it is so possessive as to cause distress through jealousy, but gradually, after experience and development, the sympathies expand, and eventually reach out to enfold all humanity. It has been said by wise spiritual teachers that the power of a mother's love, rightly directed, can create a circle of light and protection around her child sufficient to shield it from all harm, no matter to what dangers it is exposed.

In fairytale symbolism, the influence of Cancer, and the lesson it teaches, is that of the magic garden, surrounded by a high wall, within which the joys of summer eternally abound. Such gardens are frequent in myth and fairytale. Each of us can and should create our own garden, for all people, particularly those learning the lesson of this sign, need some sanctuary where they can find rest and recuperation. On the outer plane, the home supplies this need, and for this reason we are taught that the home should be sacred and beautiful, a storehouse of power which will nourish and recreate its inmates. Unfortunately, perhaps owing to the karma incurred by breaking spiritual laws in the past, not every home is thus sanctified; but nothing can prevent any soul from building within its own being its own quiet refuge, its magic garden. Steady control of the thoughts and emotions will secure the walls and the tenacity of purpose characteristic of Cancer will maintain the soul. All children of Cancer have the power of creative imagination to a greater or lesser degree, and should make a daily habit of using this creative power to visualize a truly magic garden where the sun shines, where the birds sing, and where there is a quiet pool upon which blooms a beautiful pure white water-lily—a garden of tranquillity and eternal summer. If a few minutes are spent daily in creating this garden within the consciousness, it will soon become a reality, and its strong walls will protect the soul from all inharmony.

The actual effect of this practice will be to create a circle of light and protection around the sensitive psychic vehicle. Thus, instead of being swayed and battered by every astral influence, harmonious or otherwise, the soul will open to the divine sunlight and the psychic faculties will quicken to catch the messages from the heaven world.

With perseverance and regular practice, this spiritual aspiration will gradually give rise to an abiding inward tranquillity, which will impart strength and radiance to the soul. Wherever it goes, the peace of the magic garden will enfold it, and the emotions, purified and blest by the sunshine within, will flow out to heal and enfold those in need of sympathy and sustenance. The Master Jesus said to his disciples, *Feed my sheep*. This aspect of the soul, reflected by the sign of Cancer, when fully developed gives that tender, protective maternal love and compassion which can succour and feed humanity.

LEO

The sign of Leo, coming directly under the influence of the Sun, its ruler, has long been known as the 'royal sign', for it bestows on its children the vitality, warmth, radiance and willpower which make them natural leaders. The Sun enters this sign around July 23rd each year, and during the month following, summer is still at its height. It is interesting that many of the flowers which bloom in English gardens at this period display the flaming gold, orange, and warm tawny colours which belong to the sign of Leo; interesting also that August is the children's holiday month, since in the horoscope Leo is associated with the fifth house, ruling children and pleasure as well as love affairs and speculation.

In Leo, the element Fire manifests in its fixed quality, and if we can by the exercise of our imaginative powers correlate the characteristics of a steadily-glowing fire (or of the Sun itself) to human life and conduct, we shall gain an idea of the nature of the sign. Children of Leo respond simply and unquestioningly to the dictates of a warm, ardent, impulsive heart, which is the mainspring of their activities. All the Fire signs stimulate and intensify the affections, but Leo, which rules the heart centre, is preeminently the sign whose influence unfolds consciousness of the power of love as the controlling centre of the universe.

Within the heart of everyone is the spark of God, which must eventually wax and glow until it becomes first a steady flame and finally a glorious star or sun. This spark of God, the infant Christ established within the heart, is influenced and guided by each zodiacal sign in turn. In the process of its education, sometimes the 'child' must struggle so hard with the limitations of matter that it can find small opportunity for full expression of its powers, while at other times it is given more freedom.

When the soul incarnates under the influences of Leo, it has reached a period during which the Christ, or the Sun within the heart, is allowed some freedom of expression, and can demonstrate in creative work how well it has assimilated its previous lessons. Always, the human heart has direct access to the divine Light, the Source of life; but not always can this power be brought through into physical manifestation. When we are born strongly influenced by Leo, however, our whole being is set to obey the dictates of the heart, and during that incarnation the spirit has an opportunity for creative self-expression.

The fact of being consciously or unconsciously *en rapport* with the heart of the universe gives to the soul a sense of security and self-confidence, so that it does not need to look to human authority in action and belief. In fact, it usually objects to doing so, and only feels happy when allowed to work on its own initiative. Children of Leo are never so contented as when working out an idea or project in their own way, and in so doing draw around themselves a band of helpers who, fired by their leader's enthusiasm, and under his or her instruction, are willing to undertake various aspects of this work, particularly those connected with laborious detail. In this way the Sun power, shining through the heart, attracts to itself satellites to form a group or small universe, and rules the whole with benevolent despotism. Souls working under zodiacal influences which deny self-confidence are attracted to such natural leaders, who give them strength, support, and warm, affectionate encouragement—usually not unmixed with patronage!

The fact that the Light within the heart is stimulated and allowed expression causes children of Leo to be simple, wholehearted and sincere in whatever they undertake. The soul will thus respond to the influence of the sign, no matter what its age and experience, for the human heart is fundamentally incapable of subterfuge. The joyous sense of power and wellbeing given by this inrush of vitality and sunlight may cause a feeling of self-importance in the inexperienced soul, who may become bombastic, boastful and inclined to over-ambition.. They may act much as a child given the materials and freedom will cheerfully attempt to draw a picture that would tax the powers of a trained artist. Fully believing in its own ability, when its efforts come to nothing, the soul will be more astonished than anyone at its own failure.

This essential vitality also finds expression in the inexperienced soul through love of luxury, display and the use of gaudy colours with showy ornamentation; while the sense of inward freedom and powers of creation turn more towards pleasure and self-indulgence than to constructive work. The soul may then use its powers of leadership purely in the idle pursuit of pleasure instead of in service to humanity. Even the affection characteristic of Leo is often marred by being indiscriminately and overlavishly bestowed; the ardour and generosity of souls under the Sun's sign often overpower those who receive them. Many are the heartaches and disappointments suffered before wisdom is blended with love, and the lesson mastered.

Here it is interesting to consider the Greek myth of

Phaeton, the son of Apollo the Sun god, who claims his privilege to drive the Sun-chariot across the heavens. When this privilege is granted, he finds himself unable to control its fiery steeds, so that they bolt, and flung out of his chariot, he perishes. This story illustrates the tendency towards over-confidence in its own powers, which tempts the soul to choose the path of selfwill instead of obedience to the God-will within. When the 'child of the Sun' thus claims his or her birthright, the Sun powers released within may prove too strong for his or her control, and the creative fire is squandered in foolish self-glorification and indulgence. Instead of enthusiastic friends and co-workers, the Leo then draws around him- or herself flatterers and sycophants who will desert him or her in time of trial, and bitter is the sorrow and disillusionment that must be faced.

Leo, the sign of kingship and royal authority, teaches the soul the lesson of obedience to the God within, for it is only by itself becoming obedient to divine Will that it can learn to control the first kingdom which it must rule, the kingdom of the self. Through this aspiration, and the exercise of the divine Will, all the vehicles are gradually drawn into alignment with the magnetic forces of earth and heaven. Mind and emotions, warmed and irradiated by the divine Love, will be guided and restrained by divine Will and Wisdom;

while the physical body will manifest the harmonious government of the Fire within by its poised erect carriage and by radiant health and magnetism.

The white light of the Sun contains within itself all the colours of the rainbow; so the soul when incarnating under Leo can, according to its age and experience, understand and harmonise with each of the seven rays of progress. Apollo was patron of all the arts and sciences, and the released sun powers within the heart enable a soul successfully to devote its attention to government, teaching, science, art, healing, philosophy, or mysticism and ceremonial. However, it will always claim freedom to work independently along the lines chosen and to lead and organize those who wish to follow its example.

Children of Leo are simple-hearted, having an innate faith in God, in themselves, and in the honour and goodwill of other souls towards them. For this reason they are often hoodwinked by those unscrupulous enough to take advantage of their simplicity and somewhat artless vanity. In the inexperienced soul such deception occasions much sorrow and bewilderment and a temporary if somewhat half-hearted attempt at cynicism. However, even after such setbacks the sun soon shines again, and more wisdom has been stored for future use.

Leo teaches the soul the true meaning of love. By

means of many experiences the soul's vision increases, until it learns that while the real self, the spirit within all, is constant and trustworthy, often the outer or lower self fails. With this realization comes knowledge of its own true function as a leader, which is to search for and encourage the good, the spark of divine Fire in others; or to discover the crock of gold hidden at the end of the varied rainbow manifestations of the outer self of human kind. Thus will it find justification for its faith in the innate goodness in others; and know that however often the outer, lower self denies its master, the real self will rise again and again with renewed effort to become worthy. It then endeavours to lead and inspire by example and by unquenchable faith in the ultimate victory of that nobler self, a victory which will lead every soul through the valley of the shadow and onward into the Land of Light.

VIRGO

The traditional symbol of the sign of Virgo is the Maiden bearing in her arms a sheaf of corn. This seems particularly appropriate in the northern hemisphere where, at the period when the Sun is passing through this sign (approximately August 23rd to September 23rd), the corn harvest is being gathered.

In Virgo, the element Earth manifests in its mutable or adaptable phase. All the Earth signs teach the spirit the lesson of service; and the specialized form of this lesson, taught by the mutable phase of the element, is knowledge gained through investigation, which will in turn lead to wisdom in service. Virgo is ruled by Mercury, the planet of mind. We find that the children of the sign bring their minds to bear on the manipulation of earth (the physical life and its problems), and thus are naturally drawn to the mathematical sciences which bring matter under the control of mind. An idea or mental concept brought into physical manifestation (if only in some simple piece of carpentry) demands mathematical accuracy in its execution, if the finished product is to work smoothly and be a good representation of the mental picture.

To use the mind to shape and mould matter is instinctive with Virgo natives, as is care over detail and desire for absolute accuracy, without which it is impossible to achieve perfection. In the course of the growth and unfoldment of the spirit, one of the important lessons that must be mastered is accuracy and perfection in every detail of life. If we are eventually to become godlike, we must gradually unfold our understanding of the precision of the Law, which governs not only the motion of the planets round the Sun but also the minutest detail in the life-cycle of the smallest wayside flower. Souls coming into incarnation when the Sun is passing through Virgo are, through the Earth devas, receiving training in this quality. Much experience is needed in many life-cycles before full knowledge of the perfection of God's laws can be attained; and when the soul first attempts to learn this lesson it finds difficulty in keeping a sense of proportion.

Because of the connection of the planet Mercury with Virgo, all the children of the sign are mentally active, and constantly seek knowledge that will bring matter under the control of mind. They are drawn to all types of scientific study and often become clever and agile mentally, apt at comparison, criticism and argument. Their interest in detail causes them to subject small sections of life to microscopic analysis rather than to consider first the relationship of each part to the whole. This applies to many of their problems also, and the striving after perfection in trivialities may blind the soul to the main issues of life, causing muddle and confusion.

The human mind, while a good servant, is a bad master; and when it usurps rulership from the spirit, sorrow and anarchy reign in the kingdom of the soul. For the spirit, even when incarnating in matter, retains a memory of the illimitable, which the mind, with its limited horizons, cannot hope to share. The mind by analysis, criticism, and comparison can study the laws governing matter, and master life's practical details; but if it becomes powerful and arrogant, ignoring the promptings of the spirit, these practical details assume unwarranted importance and blind the soul to its divine destiny. The vision of heaven, which is the birthright of the spirit, can be destroyed by the process of dissection, criticism and analysis accorded to matter. Men and women cannot hope to scale the heights or plumb the depths of the infinite with their minds alone, and because of this, seek refuge in denial of their existence.

This state brings chaos and mental hell. However,

as soon as the mind acknowledges the direction and guidance of the King within, instead of being fettered and blinded, it becomes illumined and vitalized by the sunlight of the spirit. It dissects, weighs and analyses matter with quickened vision and understanding, so that where before it saw merely dry dust it now discerns living gold. Even in mathematical formulae can be discovered a hidden number, a magic key which gives the secret of transmuting base metals into fine gold.

The gift of the spirit to the mind, which faithfully obeys its dictates, is discrimination: discrimination between the essential and the trivial, the real and the unreal, the true and the false. Without this gift, the soul must wander long in the wilderness of illusion, mistaking a brilliant intellect, with its faculty of criticism, for heavenly wisdom, and becoming ever more bewildered and unhappy. Discrimination causes destructive judgments to be forgotten, for the radiant spirit shining through the mind lights up the grains of gold within the dust of earthliness; and the Christlike soul sees only the Christlike qualities in others.

In the horoscope, Virgo is associated with the sixth house, which rules service and employment as well as health. As mind should serve spirit, faithfully executing the tasks which the Master, the Sun within the universe of the soul, commands, so in the outer world the child of Virgo can express his or her gifts most harmoniously when working under the direction of a leader who will assign those tasks which require patience, precision, and exact attention to detail. This sign does not give its children self-confidence, and they are liable to become overanxious if forced to accept the responsibility of taking far-reaching decisions. Being perfectionists, they are over-critical of themselves as well as of other people. They doubt their own ability to cope adequately with difficulties which may arise and therefore vacillate and are quickly daunted by opposition. This state of fear and tension can only be overcome by the realization of divine strength. Alone, humans are powerless to achieve anything, but with God all things are possible. If mental arrogance is laid aside, and the issue humbly surrendered to divine wisdom, light and help will flow freely to that soul so that his or her powers will be adequate for the task.

The sixth house, which Virgo rules, is also the house of health. It indicates to the astrologer the state of our health, the complaints to which we are liable and our general interest in health matters. In Greek mythology, the health goddess Hygeia was often identified with the Maiden who forms the symbol of this sign; while in our own times the symbol of the medical service is the caduceus, the magic staff of Mercury, ruler of Virgo.

From these facts, it would seem that the ancient sages were well aware that the mind has an intimate and indissoluble connection with the health of the body. As the matter composing the world outside the human being must be studied, analysed and brought under the control of the mind, so also must the matter which composes the physical body. For this reason, Virgo gives its children an interest in health and hygiene. This may take a negative form, so that they are continually thinking about health, wanting a scientific knowledge of the construction of the body in order to bring it under the control of the mind. If, however, the mind in its turn is not under the control of the spirit, the interest that should lead to wise care, purity, and wholeness or holiness, leads instead to foolish fears and apprehensions which can result in semi-invalidism. Where the interest takes a positive form, we find children of Virgo drawn to the medical profession, to nursing, massage, chiropractics, nutrition and other keys to healing.

The secret of perfect health is indeed contained in the mystery of Virgo, the sign of service. Under its influence we learn that the body must serve the mind, and the mind must in humility and simplicity serve the spirit, while the spirit serves and obeys the Great Architect of the Universe. The Light of the spirit illumining the mind gives wisdom. A wise person does not wear out the body's energies with worry, fret and overwork. Such a one studies the needs of the body and is wisely moderate and discriminating in his or her demands, while not tolerating laziness or over-indulgence. When the mind serves only the Great White Spirit, it becomes tranquil and confident in the eternal love and wisdom, in the cosmic law which transmutes evil into good, and ugliness into beauty. The body in turn responds to this peaceful mental state by being relaxed and restful, yet ready for action. Thus polarized, the whole being is open to the universal life-force, which can flow through every vehicle, cleansing, purifying, healing and recreating, so that the soul can indeed worship the Lord in the beauty of holiness.

In myth and fairytale, we may compare the Virgin of the zodiac to the pure and innocent princess whom the knight (the human spirit) with a magic sword of light must rescue from the monsters of ignorance and arrogance. The golden sheaves she carries are the sheaves of wisdom garnered in the fields of experience; for purity is neither the blindness of ignorance nor the fear of contamination. It is full and comprehensive knowledge, transmuted by the power of love into the simplicity of wisdom. The soul thus cleansed and clad in a garment whiter than snow, approaches the mystery of life—no longer with criticism and doubt, but with a childlike wonder and reverence. It sees in all things a manifestation of divine love, truth, and beauty; and knows that the humblest service to the least of God's creation is an act of praise, of worship, and of thankfulness to the Most High.

LIBRA

Astrology or spiritual science teaches that the cycle of experience symbolized by the circle of the zodiac begins at the point known as 0° Aries. In actual fact, of course, a circle has no beginning and no end, but if we have the concept of life evolving in a spiral, it is easy to understand how a fresh cycle (or circle) of the spiral begins at 0° Aries. That is why, traditionally, the day on which the Sun reaches this point (either March 21st or 22nd) is known as the first day of spring. This date marks the spring equinox.

Usually on September 23rd, at the time of the autumn equinox, the Sun enters the sign of Libra, at which point it has completed a half-yearly cycle, and may be said to be beginning the return journey. During the following six months every sign through which the Sun will pass will complement or balance one of those in the first half of the zodiac.

This tendency towards balance, harmony and completion is inherent in Libra. Its function in the divine scheme is indicated by its symbol, the Scales of Justice, which represent the law of equilibrium, one of the five fundamental spiritual Laws by which human kind is governed.

Libra is the second of the Air signs, showing the element in its cardinal or active phase. We may compare it to a steady breeze or current of air, which winnows the wheat from the chaff. This is precisely the action of the sign: to sift and balance the elements in the human soul, to mould and bring it to beauty and perfection.

In previous chapters we have noted that the element Air is concerned with the development of the mental vehicles. Souls coming strongly under its influence live in the mind rather than the feelings and sensations. Libra is ruled by Venus, the planet of beauty, harmony and symmetry, and consequently its children tend to exercise their mental gifts in the pursuit of beauty. Unlike natives of the other Venusian sign, Taurus, they tend to seek a mental rather than a physical appreciation and perception of beauty. They delight in comparison and judgment, and possessing a natural sense of proportion, have an intuitive ability to strike the balance between two sides of an argument. They do not prove good fighters or advocates for any particular line of thought, for the simple reason that they clearly see both its advantages and disadvantages, and instinctively take the path of compromise and moderation.

Air signs teach humanity the lesson of brotherhood; and while Gemini teaches this lesson through the attainment of knowledge and wisdom, the cardinal sign of Libra teaches brotherhood through action. Gemini rules brothers, sisters and cousins, the companionship of whom we must accept in childhood and youth regardless of our tastes and wishes. This is the first lesson of brotherhood. Libra takes us a step further. Through the desire for harmony and balance which it gives, we seek in a partner the qualities we lack, so that we can ourselves find completion and symmetry. Deep lessons of give and take, of balance and equilibrium in human relations come to the soul through the experiences thus gained. The child of Libra instinctively feels the unity of all life, and has no desire to work in splendid isolation. Companionship and partnership are a need almost as fundamental to it as breathing. In seeking a partner or a mate, however, the soul is often brought up against another lesson in human relations, which is linked with this sign, that of rivalry or enmity. This lesson helps us eventually to develop those qualities of justice, mercy, tolerance, gentleness and long-suffering which every soul must gain. Through it comes realization of the equilibrium and dispassion which must be attained before the soul can live in harmony, not only with its immediate associates, but with every aspect of God's universe.

The influence of Venus, ruling planet of Libra, gives the soul gentleness, affection, harmony, and an intense desire for beauty and peace, with which are combined a keen perception and an unerring instinct for pouring oil on troubled waters. There will in fact be a desire to avoid friction or inharmony at all costs.

Despite the influence of Venus in stimulating the affections, we must remember that Libra is of the Air element, and therefore the mind will tend to govern the emotions. The young soul under this influence is seldom deeply affected emotionally. Because it is not torn by its feelings, it is able to gravitate calmly and apparently without qualms of conscience to the most comfortable spot, regardless of ties of affection, should these conflict with its desires. Because of this lack of emotional depth, it is not entirely loyal either to people or ideas, and, like the Vicar of Bray in the old verse, is able to suit itself to the needs of the moment, keeping one eye on the main chance. So long as the surface of life remains smooth and pleasant it is satisfied, sweet-tempered and equable, and rarely loses this amiability because at the first hint of disturbance or harshness it quietly withdraws.

As the soul gains experience, however, its horizon widens. The quick mental perceptions, the gentleness,

and the love of beauty become directed away from itself towards others. It then becomes a real peacemaker,
because the influence of Libra gives an intuitive perception of the underlying concord in apparently conflicting
viewpoints of others. It also gives the ability, by exercise
of gentleness, patience and tact, to bring the opposing parties into agreement. That quality which in the
younger soul manifested as disloyalty, in the advanced
soul becomes dispassion; its outlook is too wide and
universal to be bounded by the prejudices or opinions
of loved ones or confederates. The one desire of the
soul is to see balance, justice, equity and brotherhood
expressed in human relations, and its actions will be impartially devoted to these ends, no matter how bitter the
criticism or resentment it incurs from partisans of any
faction, creed or nation. For this reason, the advanced
child of Libra is of utmost value to the government of
any nation, particularly when diplomacy and vision
are needed.

In this connection, it is interesting to note that the
planet Saturn, which has much to do with government
and organization, is exalted (that is to say it finds particularly harmonious expression) when passing through
the sign of Libra. This planet is usually regarded as a
malefic influence, and its effect upon any department
of life is viewed with apprehension by many astrologers.

This is because it is intimately concerned with the administration of the law of karma, or the law of cause and effect, which again has a marked bearing on the mystery of Libra. In ancient Egyptian teachings, every soul after death had to appear before the god Tahuti and be weighed in his scales to ascertain whether the good in his or her soul completely balanced the negative or bad qualities; or in other words, whether it had balanced or discharged all karmic debts. Had it done so, it was able to pass onwards to initiation and to the Land of Light, freed from the wheel of rebirth. However, if the scales were unbalanced by so much as a feather's weight, then the soul after a period of rest had to return to earth and undergo through the influence of Tahuti (or Saturn) the further experience needed to bring to it perfect balance and beauty.

This testing of the soul is represented in many ways in fairytales of all nations, tales originally designed to tell of the harmony and perfection which must be gained before people could live 'happily ever after.' Into this category fall the stories where in order to win the hand of the princess, or to inherit his father's kingdom, the prince (usually the youngest of a family of three, seven, nine or twelve children) must go forth on a quest which appears almost impossible to attain—such as to find material so fine that an hundred yards of it will pass easily through the eye of a needle; or discover a dog so small that it will sit easily within a walnut shell. We usually notice that the youngest prince wins the prize, an indication perhaps that it is the last of many incarnations (or of many efforts) which finally brings success. In addition, the youngest prince usually finds what he wants, not only because of his own vigour and courage, but through his kindly consideration and sympathy which earn the gratitude of people or creatures seemingly too humble to be helpful. These ungainly and insignificant companions often prove to be bewitched fairy princesses who can give him what he needs to pass the test.

These stories have a significance for all, but particularly for those born under the influence of Libra; for they have reached a stage on their evolutionary path when they are offered an opportunity to pass a deep spiritual test, that of absolute justice and dispassion. Like the prince, they seek a treasure most difficult to find, the jewel of perfect truth. While in the physical body, we are swayed by ideas and opinions, desires and emotions, petty foibles and prejudices. Most of us are pulled hither and thither by each new diversion that attracts or repels us; but souls learning the lesson of Libra possess the gift, if they will use it, of finding the point of balance, the 'middle way' so often referred to in eastern philosophy, which brings them to truth. The difficulty is that although the soul may perceive absolute truth and justice, it often undergoes much before it dares to abide by the truth it knows; for to be dispassionate, balanced and just in one's dealings with all people, all the time, requires selflessness and courage of no mean order. So intense must be the soul's love and loyalty towards God, the One in many forms, the Truth, the Light, the Life behind all creation, that unkindness, injustice or disloyalty to any living thing becomes impossible, because it means unkindness, injustice or disloyalty to God. In the fairytales, the prince who discovers beauty in the apparently mean and hideous and stands by what he has found , is the one who passes the test and wins the prize.

Thus, the soul striving to learn the lesson of Libra must train itself to weigh every problem in the scales of truth within the temple of its own being; it must endeavour, when the voice of conscience has revealed the truth, to follow that guidance regardless of cost. For only as the soul dares to be loyal to the truth within and behind all outward manifestation; only as it works selflessly and impartially to bring about unity and brotherhood, can it be weighed in the Balance of Tahuti and not be found wanting by so much as a feather's weight. It can then pass onwards, fearless and free, through the portals of initiation into the Land of Light.

Blessed are the peacemakers: for they shall be called the children of God.

SCORPIO

Scorpio, the eighth sign of the zodiac, is perhaps the most difficult of all to understand, since it is associated with the deepest mysteries of life. It can be comprehended only superficially by those who have not yet realized that Spirit is the great power and the life behind all manifestations of matter. The sign is symbolized by three symbols: the Scorpion, the Serpent and the Eagle—the last of the three being also the symbol of the beloved disciple, St. John. To him it was given to behold the mysteries of creation from the beginning of time, and to record these mysteries in the Book of Revelation, the meaning of which will be more clearly revealed to humanity as the new age of Aquarius advances and the mystical teaching of St John becomes the religion of the new age.*

The Sun travels through the sign of Scorpio approxi-

*The reader may be interested to refer to two books of White Eagle's teaching on this matter, THE LIVING WORD OF ST JOHN and THE LIGHT BRINGER (White Eagle Publishing Trust, 2000, 2001).

mately between October 24th and November 22nd, the period of the year when in the northern hemisphere vegetation fades and decays and all creatures prepare for the winter months; when the forces of life have given place to those of death and destruction. In the horoscope, Scorpio is associated with the eighth house, which rules decay and regeneration, and for this reason is regarded by many as a somewhat gloomy sign. Mars, the planet which rules Aries, also rules Scorpio: the Sun's passage through the former brings manifestations of new life and energy to the physical plane; and through the latter, destruction, or rather a transmutation of energy from the outer to the inner planes of being.

Also associated with this sign is Pluto, God of the underworld, who in Greek mythology stole away Persephone, goddess of spring. Students nowadays believe this myth to refer solely to the destruction by winter of all the fresh young life which spring had brought into being; but a deeper significance is attached, since every drama enacted within the cosmos is also enacted within the human soul. The smaller is a mirror of the happenings of the larger, and the larger of the infinite. Hermes said, 'As above so below, as below so above': this is why the observant soul needs no books to teach it the truths of God, for it sees them plainly written in every phase of life and nature.

What is this mystery of Pluto, God of the Under-world—of winter, of death, of regeneration—which the soul learning the lesson of Scorpio must strive to comprehend? Scorpio is the sign of desire in all its forms, from the basest and most material to the final all-consuming desire for at-one-ment with God, which has animated and inspired all the great saints the world has ever known. Both the Martian signs are signs of desire, for Mars itself is the planet of desire. Desire motivates our lives; it gives us strength and energy to perform our tasks, to strive for the attainment of our wishes. The intense desire or need of the spirit for manifestation on the outer planes causes the outrush-ing of life-forces associated with spring and with the sign of Aries.

When this full expression has been accomplished, there comes a corresponding desire for deeper realiza-tion, for fuller understanding than can ever be attained through matter alone. Thus in Scorpio, the sign of se-crets, we find the desire to penetrate to the heart, to the secret place, which eventually leads a soul back to reality, to God. In the course of this search, the soul must come up against the mystery of the death of material form and of all material desire. Usually we must experience loss and destruction of the form of that which we love before we will cease to identify ourselves with the unreal, before we can discover the root which produces the rose, or the well from which the waters of life spring.

Scorpio is a sign of the Water element manifesting its fixed phase.... The still, deep, cool water within the well which refreshes the weary traveller, which cleanses and heals. It is the dank, weed-grown, mosquito-infested water of some stagnant pool teeming with lowly forms of life ... the still waters of a deep blue lake, tranquilly reflecting the surrounding hills and trees, and the shadows of the clouds as they scud across the sky.... All these are pictures associated with different phases of the sign of Scorpio. Their lesson for its children is peace of spirit, which may be attained through an understanding of the mysteries of life and death.

The Water element rules the emotional and psychic aspect of our being, and the three Water signs make their children impressionable and sensitive. Since Scorpio is the sign of fixed or still water, souls coming under its influence tend to hide their feelings under a calm and unruffled exterior. Even the least experienced are able to exercise control over themselves if they wish, so that only an intuitive and practised student of human nature can fathom what is going on behind the barrier of calm reserve they adopt. This very silence and outward calm gives to the soul working under Scorpio a power and determination, a driving force in anything it undertakes, for silence preserves and concentrates power. In the young and inexperienced soul, this quality takes the form of secretiveness and cunning. Instinctively it realizes that silence can protect and conserve schemes dear to its heart, and so it works in an apparently underhand manner. By subtlety, secret scheming and plotting it will gain its object, taking its more open-hearted opponent completely by surprise.

There is immense power in still water. Silent and magnetic, it mirrors the activity of the world around it, yet remains unruffled and untouched, for all is reflection, illusion of reality; yet within these depths is the secret of creation. The first forms of life appear in still water, in the minute single-celled amoeba. In the human soul, the most evolved life-form manifesting on earth, the organs of creation and generation come under the influence of this tranquil Water sign.

The mystery of Scorpio is the mystery both of the creation and destruction of bodily form, of generation and regeneration. To gain understanding of this mystery is to gain the wisdom of the gods. Before reaching this goal, however, the soul must learn so to control the turbulent emotions and transmute selfish desire that it becomes as tranquil and serene as the waters of a lake on a summer's day. Reserve and self-control on the outer planes are only the beginning, yet a promise of control over the whole being which must and will eventually be reached. Once these are attained, the soul has only one desire, that of serving the Great Architect of the Universe in the way which He–She wills. Then, when the heart is tranquil, the secrets and mysteries of the universe begin to unfold; wisdom reveals itself to the soul as clearly as the sun, sky, clouds, moon and stars are mirrored in the surface of the lake.

Of the three symbols of the sign, the scorpion represents the lowest phase through which the soul must pass in the early stages of its evolution, when it is at the mercy of its over-intense desire nature. The scorpion is a creature which crawls in the dust. At this stage of development, all the soul's desires are of the earth, the young soul having no vision beyond the material plane. Its emotional power gives it strength, thoroughness and determination to gain what it wants, while the timidity characteristic of all the Water signs, coupled with the love of secrecy inherent in Scorpio, helps it to work subtly and effectively. Against any attempt to injure it or thwart its desires the soul defends itself with the virulent sting of the scorpion, which may even find outlet in physical violence when it manifests as jealousy, envy, resentment, spite and hatred. Not only does the love of secrecy show in the urge for privacy in its own affairs, but curiosity about the secrets of others is also present. Often we find children of Scorpio interested in detective or secret service work.

When, after suffering repeatedly the loss or destruction of possessions and pleasures, the soul yearns to discover the reason why, the second or Serpent aspect of the sign is reached. In this, instead of the love of secret things being focused purely on the material life, it turns towards those mysteries which can lead the soul eventually to initiation. At this stage, it is irresistibly drawn to all types of occultism; for it cannot find mental rest until it has solved to some extent at least the mystery of life and death and the purpose of existence. The soul begins to control and use the acute sensitivity which caused it to react so violently to the smallest threat of hurts and slights. It becomes aware of hidden powers in the universe, and of an inner life permeating and enriching outer forms. Furthermore, it begins to feel the suffering of others. When this happens, the children of Scorpio long to gain the wisdom that will help them to heal others, and we find many healers, doctors, and surgeons under this sign.

With increasing knowledge and wisdom, the soul makes valiant attempts to overcome and rein in the turbulent emotions and desires of the lower self. With all the strength and will of its being it fights the dragon of selfishness. In our fairytales the hero challenges the dragon or monster coiled round the well of the water of life; for only when the dragon is subdued and mastered can the victor reach into the depths to draw up a draught of the pure water and drink of immortality. The monster symbolizes the serpent fire, kundalini, coiled in the creative centre at the base of the spine, which is the mainspring of human animal energy and instinctive life. When the character and divine will become sufficiently developed to exercise control, this fire rises up the spine until it reaches the head centre. A tremendous and subtle creative force is thus released and brought under the control of the spirit, to be used in the service of God. With this transmutation of physical desire into selfless devotion comes spiritual vision and illumination; so that the soul is no longer bound to the illusions of life and death, of time and space, for all becomes one, all is God, all is eternal life.

Then, powers of true mediumship or seership are unfolded, and the sensitivity of the element Water, blending with the positive Fire of Mars, gives the balance necessary for maintaining contact between the outer and the inner worlds. At this stage the freed soul can soar, as on the wings of a white eagle, into the sunlight of the higher spheres of life: where, like St. John, it beholds the revelation of the mystery of human evolution. This is initiation, towards which all are striving; and which comes to us through battle with the monster of the lower self lying coiled round the well, withholding from us the water of life. Scorpio symbolizes this struggle, and the final attainment, through self-sacrifice and devotion, to the still, deep waters of eternal peace.

SAGITTARIUS

Sagittarius, the ninth sign of the zodiac, belongs to the element Fire, which here manifests in its mutable or variable phase. Its symbol is a centaur: a being with a man's head and torso on the body of a horse. The man aims an arrow heavenwards. This winged arrow, pointing towards the stars, represents the sign when we erect a horoscope, and typifies the innate qualities of those learning the lesson of Sagittarius.

As previously stated, souls born when the Sun is passing through a fire sign have returned to earth in order to learn more fully the lesson of love. Those born between approximately November 22nd and December 22nd fall into this category. According to their soul capacity and experience, they are learning through aspiration to blend human love with the divine. The mutable quality of the sign indicates that here the fire element does not manifest as a steady roaring flame carrying all before it (as in the sign of Aries), nor in the glowing fire which warms and comforts (as in Leo), but as the bright, fitful flame which waxes and wanes. When the flame glows, everything is illumined and beautified, and when it disappears all seems doubly dark. In the same way, when moments of aspiration bring the soul into conscious contact with God, difficulties and shadows disappear. The soul is filled with faith, hope and trust which are the natural attributes of the higher or God-self. It sees the path clearly and knows that all is good, that there is nothing to fear. Then, suddenly, the light flickers and dies, and the soul enters again the darkness of doubt and despondency.

All children of Sagittarius will feel conscious of this rhythmic pull, first of the higher and then of the lower mind, even if they are only 'young' souls. The sign stands opposite to Gemini in the zodiacal circle, and all signs opposite to each other are to some extent linked. Thus Gemini (the Twins) is preeminently the sign under which the lower mind develops through its experience of the two opposing forces of good and evil.

Sagittarius is above all concerned with the development of the higher mind through its experience of the two extremes of exaltation and despondency. The soul is alternately conscious of the inflow of the divine love and light through its whole being, and of darkness and despondency when the pull of earth appears to deny its bright hopes and visions. During its darkness the soul learning this lesson gradually becomes conscious of an inward, unquenchable spirit of hope which strengthens with every effort to soar; and causes all Sagittarians, no matter what their stage of development, to be at heart invincible optimists. As is to be expected, however, the more inexperienced the soul, the less it will inquire into the true significance of its higher moments.

The dual nature of the sign is well portrayed in its symbol, half man, half horse. The untamed horse loves to roam far and wide, grazing, galloping and neighing with the sheer joy of being alive. It is difficult to catch, and until broken and well-trained will prove an unreliable servant. This somewhat irresponsible aspect manifests clearly in the inexperienced children of Sagittarius. They are cheerful and good-natured, filled with *joie de vivre*, but they quickly shy away from responsibility, and would preserve their personal freedom at all costs. Their exuberant energy quickens their interest in all kinds of physical activity and sport, while an innate restlessness makes them desire travel and constant change.

When, because of inexperience or wilfulness, the soul responds only to the animal aspect of the sign, the higher aspect, represented by the man aiming his arrow upward, lies dormant. Occasional flashes of intuition or foreknowledge which, if cultivated, could bring true guidance in the science of life, are recognized only as 'lucky hunches' which bring success on the material plane. Since neglected gifts atrophy through disuse, if the young Sagittarian refuses to respond to the higher self, and makes no effort to check his or her irresponsibility, this intuitive power will gradually cease to function. Then, like a rudderless ship, the soul will drift with the tide, driven hither and thither, partly by circumstance and partly by its own restless enthusiasms. In the same way, Fire in its mutable or variable phase alternately flares up and is spent.

Gradually, however, the soul tires of physical freedom when there is no spiritual surety behind it, and comes to realize that it can travel all over the world without ever escaping from its limitation, loneliness and frustration.

When this realization comes, the search begins for the freedom of the spirit; and with this search the influence of the other aspect of the sign, that of the man shooting his arrow towards the stars, comes into play. The energy which once found boisterous expression in physical activity is gradually redirected to the pursuit of spiritual and mental aims. The desire to rove the world becomes transmuted into desire to explore the riches of the kingdoms within the self. The love of the chase developed by sport, games, and athletics, is now devoted to the pursuit of wisdom, to scientific, philosophic and metaphysical study. The interest in sport widens into a desire to abide by the laws governing life. Thus the unruly animal, the lower or personal self, is trained to serve in its right place and is master no longer.

When efforts are made to this end, there comes a deep desire for divine love, for contact with the higher self; and with this yearning and aspiration the intuition awakens. Often a flash of inspiration will illumine the soul, so that with the swiftness of an arrow it finds the solution to some problem without recourse to the laborious reasoning process characteristic of the opposite sign, Gemini. It is not easy, at first, for the soul to distinguish between true intuition and an active imagination, so that sometimes it jumps to faulty conclusions. Therefore, although the child of Sagittarius naturally likes to cover a wide field in a short space of time, he or she must exercise concentration and self-control in order scientifically to check each step, and to ensure accuracy. Otherwise there will be much diffusion of thought, with resultant confusion. Concentration and patience do not come easily to the Sagittarian, yet without this self-discipline, the fullest use can never be made of his or her fine intelligence and inspirational faculties.

The planet ruling Sagittarius is Jupiter, the planet of growth and expansion, the beneficent lawgiver of the heavens. Thus, one of the lessons this sign teaches the soul is that of working in harmony with the law of life on all planes, since only thus can true freedom be found.

When through self-discipline and effort, the soul begins to conserve and wisely direct its energies, instead of impulsively dissipating them, it responds more fully to the subtler influences of Jupiter. The higher mind begins to unfold and becomes increasingly active. Gradually the soul ceases to be bound by material limitations. It becomes conscious of the true meaning of religion, which is the awareness of God in everything. This harmonizes and illumines first the soul's own life, and then, by example and infection, the lives of others. Other souls will instinctively turn to it for guidance and help along the path heavenward.

The true function of the advanced Sagittarian is to be guide, philosopher, friend and lawgiver to his or her companions. When the children of Sagittarius have found truth for themselves, they will speak words of consolation, wisdom and inspiration, and the light of love will shine through their lives to help and guide others in need of help. As in the Greek myths the heroes were sent in their youth to the wise old centaur to be trained in the science of life, so will the young heroes of the soul's quest for freedom be drawn to those who have well and truly learnt the lesson of Sagittarius. In this way they too may learn how to unlock the riches of the higher mind and find the freedom of the higher worlds, so that by aspiration and self-discipline they may enter the Elysian fields.

CAPRICORN

Saturn, the planet closely associated with old age, rules Capricorn, the sign through which the Sun passes approximately between December 22nd and January 21st. Souls with this sign strongly emphasized in their horoscopes often appear to have been 'born old.' They take life and its responsibilities very seriously, and sometimes seem to be weighed down with care. The year itself is getting old when the Sun enters this sign, and everybody begins to look back, to check up on past experiences and mistakes.

Souls born under Capricorn manifest the deliberation which generally characterizes old age. They never act impulsively, but always with premeditated care, and strictly in accordance with existing rules and regulations. They entertain respect for authority, and would not dream of disobedience. When in charge of any concern, they see that rules are punctiliously observed, sometimes displaying an inflexibility which becomes absurd.

To them a rule is a rule: and any infringement,

no matter for what cause, must be reprimanded and punished. Thus they mete out justice, sometimes untempered with mercy or common sense. They not only cherish a deep respect for law, order and convention, but also reverence all that is ancient. They are interested in ancient habits and customs, in traditional usages, and feel that the wisdom of antiquity can supply much that is useful for present-day conduct. They enjoy visiting old buildings and places of historical interest and may collect antiques. All this, when the soul is young in experience, may cause a pharisaical attitude of mind which obeys the letter of the law rather than the spirit.

When the soul reaches this phase in evolution, it has arrived at a point where it must meet and master the temptations of matter. Capricorn is a sign which comes under the element Earth in its cardinal or active phase, and as the child of the Sun enters this influence it encounters the powers of the material plane in all their force and subtlety. Since it is endowed with a practical and energetic outlook, hard work, concentration upon and the solution of material problems form its only real interest. Knowledge of practical issues is one of the gifts of Capricorn. Often this aspect of life so absorbs the consciousness that memory of dependence upon the divine source of supply vanishes.

In the northern hemisphere, the Sun's entry into

Capricorn marks the traditional beginning of winter. Under the influence of this sign, the soul feels itself cut off from the warmth of the spiritual Sun; since matter appears to be the only reality, it is tempted to disregard as impractical anything that has not an immediate and apparent material significance.

Being thus earthbound, the soul will feel a keen inner sense of isolation and want. The child brought up to believe in Father Christmas feels disappointment on learning that this story is only symbolical of the Christmas spirit. So also, the soul confronted by the hard facts of matter feels for the time empty and bereft. It has lost the vision of the beauty of the spirit and the love of the Father–Mother, and forgets that all we possess comes from God and will return to God. Worry, anxiety, and fear of loss, give the child of Capricorn a heavy load to bear, and his or her serious expression and economical, prudent habits reflect this. Material security means a great deal to the children of Capricorn. For this they will work, plan and sacrifice unflinchingly. Their sense of responsibility makes them thorough, painstaking and careful. They are neat, precise, punctual and methodical in the execution of their work.

Capricorn is the last of the Earth signs, and under its influence, power and understanding of the laws of matter can reach the zenith. Material science, politics, business management, organization and government officialdom are most congenial to Capricornians, and their concentration, perseverance and hard work must bring them recognition in time, usually—again the influence of Saturn—from those older than themselves, or exercising authority over them.

The symbol of Capricorn is the mountain goat, or (an older symbol still) the Unicorn, whose one horn represents the one-pointedness of the children of this sign. Once they have set themselves an aim in life, no matter what it is, they work unremittingly, and, if young and inexperienced, often unscrupulously, to attain recognition and acknowledgment, either in social, business, political, intellectual or occult affairs. Always children of Capricorn possess this innate urge to struggle and to climb, nor are they deterred by obstacles. Indeed, their realism shows them that there is much to be overcome; and usually they tend to exaggerate rather than minimise the difficulties. They are often of a melancholy turn of mind, although they never doubt their power to achieve their end.

Here souls working under Capricorn come up against perhaps their greatest lesson. The zest for, and the battle with matter are apt to give them too great a faith in its power and in their own personal ability to cope with any problem or situation which may arise. They grow wise with the wisdom of the world. Their experience of human frailty, coupled with an innate desire for law, order and perfection, tend to make them cynical and suspicious, hard and merciless, but nevertheless just in their dealings with others. They are impatient of anything which does not come strictly under the heading of practical and sensible; and confident of their own ability. With all this weight of wisdom and experience in the brain, the heart is cold and empty. Pride of intellect and material power appear to rule, while the Sun, the light within the heart, seems dead.

As surely as the winter solstice heralds the return of life and spring, so at this point something happens which marks the winter solstice of the soul's experience—some sudden downfall which brings about destruction of pride, when all that once appeared stable and permanent crumbles to dust. At this moment all that has been gained seems as nothing. The soul at last realizes its own emptiness and impotence, and from the darkness of despair cries for help. Some old and long-forgotten memories stir and waken, and in a flash comes understanding of the need for God. With all the strength of its being the soul, like a prodigal son, calls upon God. As this cry goes forth, within the stony cave of the heart shines a ray of divine sunlight; and Love, humble, gentle and simple, is born, the Christ babe within the manger. Although the world of its material ambitions may lie in ruins, the soul no longer cares; for now, inwardly kneeling, it worships the newborn babe, and listens enraptured to the eternal song of the angels.

Once this realization has dawned, the true meaning of the sign of Capricorn begins to be understood. All the Earth signs teach the lesson of service; and the soul realizes that none of its work and effort to reach perfection has been in vain. The purpose of life is not that the soul should escape from harsh reality; but that the Christ within should control and dominate life, not for any gratification of self, not in the hope of personal acclamation, but that God may be glorified. For this reason the soul does not cease its efforts. Rather, it works more diligently than before. Never again, however, in arrogance and self-sufficiency, for it has recognized a law greater, a purpose finer than that of selfish struggle for power, wiser than all worldly wisdom. A selfless love and simple trust in God shines in the heart, and from this time onwards illumines every action, enabling the beauty and perfection of God to be expressed in matter. No longer is the soul bowed with responsibility and worry, for it knows that the Father–Mother holds all things within His–Her divine plan, and that nothing can go awry. Serenity and joy take the place of fret and melancholy, and life is lived calmly and philosophically.

Many astrologers teach that Capricorn is the sign of the Priest–Initiate. This indeed is the highest expression of the attributes of the sign. For when by self-discipline, training and struggle, the physical body has been prepared; when the trials and temptations to selfishness on all planes have been mastered; when the heart is filled with pure and simple love; then that soul can become a focus point for the Wisdom, the Love, and the Power of God. These qualities pour through it, as a living stream of light to heal, to bless and to consecrate. It then fulfils the highest function and obligation of priesthood.

AQUARIUS

Owing to the phenomenon known as the precession of the equinoxes, the world comes under the influence of a different sign of the zodiac for successive periods of roughly two thousands years. The whole zodiacal cycle, or Great Year, takes about 26,000 years to complete, during which time all the twelve signs in turn hold sway over human destiny, and many civilizations rise and fall. In this Great Year, however, the signs appear to be succeeding each other in the opposite direction to that of the 'little year'. We are now passing out of the Age of Pisces, and entering the Age of Aquarius. Consequently, at the present time this sign is of as much general as personal interest to students of the occult.

During the whole cycle, Wise Ones watch over humanity's progress, sometimes taking an active part in guiding material affairs, yet sometimes withdrawing to the inner planes, leaving humanity to learn through experience how to bring through into physical manifestation the harmony of the spirit.

During periods when the positions of power in the world have been occupied by sages and initiates, the coming of a new age has been foreseen, and the minds of the people have been prepared for the fresh influence which would be operating. In this way, the transition period has been accomplished without the great upheavals and bloodshed marking our present transition period. The effects of the approaching sign begin to be felt some time before it is actually in power, since the beginning of one sign merges with the end of its forerunner, and as in all aspects of nature, there is no distinct line of demarcation of influence, but rather a gentle merging.

Perhaps the first faint stirrings of response in the hearts of the people to this new influence were felt shortly after the discovery of Uranus in 1781; for in 1789 came the French Revolution, whose ideals of 'Liberty, Equality, Fraternity,' were distinctly Aquarian in tone. This stirring of people's hearts to human ideals coming so soon after the discovery of Uranus is interesting in view of the fact that this planet undoubtedly has a close association with Aquarius; so close indeed that astrologers regard Uranus as a co-ruler of the sign with Saturn. It is also interesting that this stirring took place in France, a country under the influence of Leo, the sign opposite and complementary to Aquarius; for the two generally manifest together. (For instance, in the preceding Age of Pisces, much stress has been laid on the Virgin birth and the celibacy of the priesthood; both of which are mysteries connected with Virgo, the complement of Pisces.)

In England first, and in other countries since, the Industrial Revolution has led to large numbers of the population being forced to abandon their handicrafts and village communities and herd together in slum cities close to mills and factories, thus creating new problems of organization and government. Today, much thought is being given to how machinery (which has come to human kind under the auspices of Uranus and Aquarius) will be so used that all people shall have the benefit of leisure, and thus find opportunity to develop their minds and follow their chosen cultural pursuits.

Aquarius is a sign of the element Air manifesting in its fixed phase, the phase of stabilization. As has been shown in previous chapters, the Air signs assist human kind to develop the mental body, and the two thousand years during which Aquarius holds sway will bring about the full development of humanity's mental stature. Discoveries yet undreamed of will be made, given to human kind by scientific and inventive geniuses born under the influence of Uranus. Further research will demonstrate the existence and use of fine ethers, the discovery of which will revolutionize medical science. Telepathy or thought-transference, and the power of thought-projection, will become common knowledge. Before the reign of Aquarius ends, it is probable that people will have regained the secret of cooperation with denizens of the elemental, nature and angelic kingdoms in the service of life.

All these, however, are of small consequence compared with the real spiritual significance of the sign. The element Air teaches the soul the lesson of brotherhood. During the Age of Aquarius worldwide brotherhood, a community not only of the mind but of the heart, will be firmly established. The qualities and functions of the human mind are such that while it can perceive the need for brotherhood, by nature it is too cold and critical to bring the ideal through into practical expression. True brotherhood can only be established through warmth of heart flowing forth in friendliness and compassion, energizing, synthesizing and bringing into full expression on all planes the ideal pictured in the mind. The instinct for such brotherhood is now stirring strongly in the heart of men and women all over the world. The true spiritual reason for the present chaos and unrest is that this new wine of the spirit cannot be contained in the outworn bottles of the Piscean Age.

As the new strong shoots push up in the spring and

thrust the old dead growth aside, so this impulse in the heart of humanity is rising to burst the old shackles and bondage.

In learning the lesson of brotherhood, many mistakes have been and probably still will be made. They will be due largely to men and women seeking brotherhood with the mind rather than the heart; but wisdom comes with experience. Teachers and leaders needed to assist humanity to respond to the requirements of the new age will, at the appointed time, come forward to guide and direct every aspect of material life. Every awakened soul, according to his or her evolution and gifts, is being used at this time to spread the gospel of the new age, the gospel of brotherly kindness and consideration for the needs of others.

Souls born under the influence of Aquarius, no matter whether the Sun was in this sign at their birth (in which case their birthdays will fall between January 21st and February 20th), or whether the sign is emphasized in some other way in their horoscopes, have special responsibilities towards the advancement of the spirit of the new age. They are psychologically in the position to understand and interpret the underlying trends of modern thought. Naturally interested in problems of science, philosophy, religion and sociology, they spend much time studying and pondering on these subjects.

The influence of Saturn in this connection gives depth and stability to the mind and increases the power of concentration. True Aquarians may remain open-minded and undecided for a long time, but once their minds are made up, they steadfastly pursue their course, undaunted by the opinions or criticism of others.

Whatever their stage of evolution, they are interested in all people, and will work with others in societies and groups for some common ideal. The child of this sign, even when young in experience on the spiritual path, intuitively aspires to some altruistic ideal and will work for it wholeheartedly. Friendship and companionship are important to an Aquarian. They usually have a happy knack of fraternizing easily with others, while a pleasant, mild and obliging disposition make them popular and well-liked. The Aquarian has a sturdy independence of outlook and a natural interest in and sympathy with human problems which readily win respect and confidence. It is rare to find the least degree of affectation or snobbery in true Aquarians, for in their sincerity and desire for truth they dislike sham and hypocrisy in any form.

Most men and women born under Aquarius respond more to the rulership of Saturn than of Uranus; the influence of the latter planet being of too subtle and fine a vibration for it to affect, except on rare occasions, souls still unawakened to the reality of spirit. Saturn is closely associated with the element Earth. Thus its influence, manifesting through the Air sign of Aquarius, is chiefly felt in the earth-mind, which becomes extremely active in children of the sign. For this reason, although they feel drawn to scientific investigation and much desire to discover truth, the power of Saturn functioning through the lower mind is inclined to limit them to that which can be perceived by the purely physical senses and limited reason. Because of this, they may miss that unchanging and enduring spiritual reality underlying all material existence. Since Aquarians when their minds are made up, are convinced of the infallibility of their opinions, this limitation can form a powerful stumbling-block to their spiritual progress. This is a danger which confronts humanity now that the Aquarian influence is becoming paramount in the world.

When this stage of intellectual deadlock has been reached, however, usually the planet Uranus, with a catastrophic lightning flash, proves itself the true friend of the human spirit. In the individual life its action will, at the appointed time, strike right across the ordered pattern of existence, causing temporary chaos and the necessity for a sudden and complete change of outlook on the mental, emotional or physical plane. Its power is irresistible; when it thus strikes, the soul has little choice but to go forward and face its destiny. It may mean the loss of all which has hitherto been held dear—personal honour, possessions, friends—and the soul will be forced to take courage in both hands and to set forth on untrodden paths with no refuge save God. At this stage, the heart centre, ruled by the complementary sign of Leo, becomes active; and the cool, dispassionate, reasoning mind begins to be balanced by the human warmth of a loving heart. Intuition awakens, and with it the ability to sense heavenly truth which formerly lay concealed from the soul's intellectual arrogance. Through this divine faculty, the soul realizes beyond any shadow of doubt that the Love of God can carry the soul unharmed through all danger. *Yea, though I walk through the valley of the shadow of death* (not merely physical death, but the apparent death of all the soul holds dear) *I will fear no evil: for Thou art with me. Thy rod and Thy staff they comfort me. Thou preparest a table before me in the presence of mine enemies. Thou anointest my head with oil; my cup runneth over. Surely goodness and mercy shall follow me all the days of my life, and I will dwell in the house of the Lord for ever.* Thus sings the soul who has faced and passed the supreme test, and found eternal truth.

The apparent chaos and destruction which the action of Uranus has made manifest in world affairs at the present time, causing nations and individuals to face this test, is now awakening the heart of humanity to essential truth. Those who are now suffering most will reap their great reward in the joy of the spiritual realization gained—and this not for one life alone, but for eternity. Truth, once having been won by suffering, can never again be lost. Like the prince in the fairytale who faced suffering and danger to reach the well of the water of life, the soul who has thus found its well of truth can carry its lifegiving waters to all.

Where are these to be found? In books? In some new order based purely on intellectual concepts of 'the good, the true, the beautiful?' These are merely outward manifestations which may mean nothing. The things of the Spirit are found in the warm, simple ways of life; in love and human kindliness, in consideration and forbearance one to another; in a tranquil assurance of God's love, and of the immortality of the soul. The child of Aquarius, who has found the living water, can bring these gifts to heal, to comfort and to sustain humanity. Through these gifts can be shown the way to a brotherhood of the heart, which alone can bring to the world the beauty and harmony of the Aquarian Age.

PISCES ♃ ♆

The sign of Pisces is perhaps one of the most interesting and yet the most misunderstood of the twelve. It comes under the element Water, manifesting in its mutable or changeable phase, and the Sun is under its influence from about February 20th to March 21st of each year. Souls born during this period have returned to earth to learn, during their present incarnation, something of the lesson of divine peace—that eternal, unchanging, dynamic stillness behind all sound, form and motion. For this they have a deep inner yearning not always recognized, which may give rise to traits difficult to understand.

As was mentioned in preceding chapters, the element Water is related to the emotions and psychic energies. Souls endeavouring to learn the lesson which it teaches are exceptionally sensitive and responsive to thoughts, feelings and astral surroundings. Since in the sign of Pisces the element manifests in its most mobile and changeable form, its children are perhaps more delicately adjusted than those of any other sign. They are so receptive that they often unconsciously absorb the ideas and mental outlook of others whom they contact, with the result that they may appear to imitate their expression and even their gestures and mannerisms. Parents and guardians of children born under this sign should be watchful that the young ones' environment consists only of influences which are helpful and worthy of imitation and absorption.

Like the sign of Aquarius, Pisces has not one but two planets so closely in harmony with it that they may be said to rule the sign. Its traditional ruler is Jupiter, the planet of compassion, which bears on the development of the higher mind and the unfoldment of spiritual consciousness. Neptune, the other ruler, brings wonderful spiritual vision and illumination to those souls ready to respond to its influence; although, as is the case with Uranus, very few men and women can be fully responsive at the present stage of human development. During the past two thousand years, when the sign of Pisces held sway, Jupiter largely influenced humanity; although the spiritual illumination of Neptune certainly touched the lives of some of the outstanding saints and visionaries of the age.

Concerned as it is with development of the higher

mind and spiritual consciousness, the material manifestation of Jupiter is closely linked with religion and churches. During the Piscean Age now passing, the culture, customs and outlook of the western civilizations have largely derived from the Church. Religious struggle and persecution have been rife; people have been discouraged by the Church from exercising reason. They have been told to accept as coming from divine authority every dictum of ecclesiastical councils and have been urged to live by faith, foregoing knowledge. Consequently, when the approaching Aquarian Age stimulated people's interest in science and invention, much of the orthodox teaching was shown to be based on superstition, and a violent revulsion followed, destroying faith, and denying much in religion that is true and beautiful and necessary to human life.

It is rare, however, for a child of Pisces to lose faith entirely, even in the present materialistic period; for even as in the sign of Sagittarius the expansive influence of Jupiter gives an unquenchable hope and optimism, so in Pisces it bestows an unconquerable faith. The stimulation of the psychic faculties also helps to break the bonds of reason; for the soul has inner experiences which convince it that more things exist in heaven and earth than material science or philosophy dreams possible.

The expansive power of Jupiter and its stimulation of the higher rather than the lower mind is apt to cause the unevolved soul to live too much in a vague dreamy state, neglecting the practical details of life. Pisceans possess a kindly, easygoing nature, and form too easily the habit of letting things drift—a trait extremely trying to their more practical brethren. It is therefore important for them to train the lower mind in concentration and the physical body in quick obedience to the dictates of the will, so that the soul can thereby express its visions and ideals on the physical plane. Unless this conscious control and direction of activity is sought, the vague, fluidic attitude of mind can cause the native to be receptive to influences from the lower astral and elemental kingdoms, confusing them with those from the higher worlds.

Traditionally Pisces is the last sign or the zodiacal circle and it symbolically represents the return of the perfected soul to the Father–Mother God. We pass through many cycles before we become at one with the infinite; each time we come to this sign on the evolutionary spiral we are conscious of an intense, almost overwhelming inward urge to reach a state of bliss, sometimes described as cosmic consciousness. While young and inexperienced, the soul does not realize the meaning of this craving—but will, nevertheless, desire to reach out, to become absorbed into something bigger than itself, to escape from natural limitations and irksome responsibilities.

Extreme sensitivity is painful in a harsh world, and therefore the soul born under Pisces needs to find some means of self-protection. At an earlier stage of evolution it may seek forgetfulness by becoming absorbed in sensation or by the effects of drink or drugs. When these methods have been exhausted and found useless, another way of escape offers: that of becoming lost in a dream world, or in fiction, where the soul can experience imaginary adventure and forget itself. This ability, if controlled and directed, may give a wonderful dramatic gift. Many of the today's stage and film stars have the sign of Pisces in some way emphasized in their horoscopes.

With growth of experience, at last the soul begins dimly to understand that its true, underlying need is for union with God. When this need is consciously realized, the soul may withdraw to a life of meditation and prayer in monastery or convent. Often, however, it does not consciously admit that it is seeking God. Nevertheless, its emotions and sympathies begin to turn outwards towards others, instead of inwards upon itself, There dawns a great tenderness and compassion for the sufferings of humanity. The overactive imagination now begins to envisage the difficulties in people's lives, and to foresee the possible hurtful effects of hasty words and actions upon the hearts of others. The soul previously absorbed in sensational experience now enters wholeheartedly into the world of human suffering and labours to bring healing and relief. It will work in the most sordid conditions, and do anything to lighten the load for others. We find children of Pisces from all levels of society devoting their strength and time to nursing, healing or missionary work in charitable institutions, prisons, asylums, or wherever the sick, the desolate and the outcast are to be found; and this with no thought of personal reward. Thus the inmost spirit begins to find that which it seeks, the secret of true heavenly peace. It learns that union with the Infinite comes only through renunciation of self.

When this understanding dawns the soul begins to respond truly to the influence of the planet Neptune. While taint of self remains, the intense spiritual power generated by Neptunian rays can only cause confusion. When, however, the lesser self becomes absorbed in service, Neptune illumines the higher mind so that the whole world becomes radiant, and even commonplace objects glow as with divine glory. This experience has come to the saints and mystics of all ages, enabling them to face derision, mockery and even death with fortitude and peace. This is the eternal beauty which artist, poet, musician and sculptor labour to express.

Pisces rules the feet, the human 'understandings'. Thus, when working under the influence of this sign, the soul is offered opportunity to gain understanding and sympathy with every phase of life, to share its joy and its suffering, its degradation and its glory.

The Master Jesus knelt to wash the feet of the disciples. So must every soul, before it can reach perfection, put aside all pride, and be ready and willing to attempt the humblest and most menial task—to live even a life of poverty and seeming degradation. The man or woman of deep spiritual power and learning may, at the bidding of the Father–Mother, renounce all and return to earth to live in poverty and obscurity. The only signs of his or her greatness will be gentleness, loving consideration and kindness to all, and patient tranquillity in the face of hardship and difficulty. Through this renunciation and joyous acceptance of lessons and hardships the soul finally reaches and becomes absorbed into the eternal peace. Nor need this necessarily be an after-death experience. The spiritual illumination of the saints (which is sometimes pictorially represented by a halo around their heads) can come to any soul during physical life; but only when the lesson of humility and renunciation taught by the sign of Pisces has been mastered.

When renunciation is so complete that no thought of self stains the purity of the soul, then is it clad in the wedding garment and bidden to the heavenly feast. Thus we see why Venus, the planet of love, union, and beauty, is said to be exalted in Pisces, symbolizing as it does the divine union, the mystical marriage of the soul. *What are these which are arrayed in white robes? ... These are they which came out of great tribulation and have washed their robes and made them white in the blood of the Lamb.*

EPILOGUE

Editorial Note

Joan Hodgson's inspiration throughout WISDOM IN THE STARS was the spirit teacher White Eagle, whose talks were given, mainly in London, week after week and sometimes more frequently. Some words of his may provide encouragement to the reader in his or her voyage of incarnation through the twelve Sun signs.

'Someone has said there seems so much to learn. I myself come back month after month, and year after year, and never can I say all I want to say. So I understand. But I shall say all I want to in due course, and you will learn all your lessons … you are learning them beautifully now. You have not the full consciousness, so you have to work blindfold; that is one of the mysteries, part of the great scheme, and where faith and trust come in. You must go on quietly, in complete trust and faith in God's love, for you know not the hour when the Son of Man cometh. This means you know not from hour to hour what glorious spiritual experience will be yours. Tonight you may be in the darkness, but tomorrow you may have received more illumination. You cannot count time. That is why faith and trust are the crowns of the humble.

'You know, my dears, I do not think it matters very much who is a great soul and who is a young soul. I do not think it matters at all. Do not worship one whom you think is great, but endeavour to love all, both great and small, young and old. Love them all … all are the same in God's sight.'

*THE WHITE EAGLE
SCHOOL OF ASTROLOGY*

Instruction in the White Eagle School of Astrology is by
correspondence course, prepared by Joan Hodgson, and
there are also regular meetings and lectures in London
and in Liss, Hampshire. The three courses are designed
to guide the student from the earliest stages to become
a professionally-qualified astrologer, and they culminate
in a Diploma examination.

BEGINNERS' COURSE

This starts from basic principles and is so simple and clear
that anyone with interest and determination can successfully calculate a chart and give a simple interpretation
by the time they finish the final lesson.

PREPARATORY COURSE

For students who already know how to calculate a chart,
these eight lessons take such students to the point at

which they are ready for the advanced course in horoscope delineation.

The advanced course in horoscope delineation makes a thorough study of the interpretative side of astrology, including rectification, vocational guidance, chart comparison, health, karma and the deeper spiritual aspects of the chart.

All necessary material (though not textbooks) is supplied with the lessons, and each student receives individual tuition. They may also use the White Eagle Lodge libraries. Further details of these lessons may be had from The White Eagle School of Astrology, New Lands, Liss, Hampshire, England, GU33 7HY, or by e-mail from astrology@whiteagle.org. For phone numbers, see over.

Readers wishing to know more of the work of the White Eagle Lodge may write to the General Secretary, The White Eagle Lodge, New Lands, Brewells Lane, Liss, Hampshire, England GU33 7HY (tel. 01730 893300) or can call at The White Eagle Lodge, 9 St Mary Abbots Place, Kensington, London W8 6LS (tel. 020-7603 7914). In the Americas please write to The Church of the White Eagle Lodge, P. O. Box 930, Montgomery, Texas 77356 (tel. 936-597 5757), and in Australasia to The White Eagle Lodge (Australasia), P. O. Box 225, Maleny, Queensland 4552, Australia (tel. 07 5494 4169).

You can also visit our websites at
www.whiteagle.org (worldwide);
www.whiteaglelodge.org (Americas);
www.whiteeaglelodge.org.au (Australasia),
www.whiteeagleca.com (Canada)

and you can email us at the addresses
enquiries@whiteagle.org (worldwide);
sjrc@whiteaglelodge.org (Americas); and
enquiries@whiteeaglelodge.org.au (Australasia).